The history of
COLWELL WOOD
and
COLWELL WOOD COTTAGE

Debrett Ancestry Research Ltd

MMXVI

ISBN: 1535099143

ISBN-13: 978-1535099141

Typeset by Debrett Ancestry Research Ltd.
PO Box 379, Winchester, SO23 9YQ, United Kingdom
Tel: +44 (0)1962 841904
www.debrettancestry.co.uk

THE HISTORY OF

COLWELL WOOD

AND

COLWELL WOOD COTTAGE

IN OFFWELL, DEVON

Gervase Belfield and Susan Morris

Commissioned by W L Hutton

Researched by Debrett Ancestry Research Ltd

CONTENTS

Preface
WILLIAM LESLIE HUTTON

William (Bill) Leslie Hutton was born on 24 July 1933 at Kirkcaldy, Scotland, and was educated at George Watson's Boys' College, Edinburgh, and at Glasgow Academy. He spent a year at Glasgow University studying mechanical engineering following an apprenticeship at Albion Motors, Scotstoun, Glasgow.

Bill Hutton has had three distinguished careers, the first being in banking. This began in April 1955 as a trainee at the Crosshill Glasgow branch of the Commercial Bank of Scotland (now part of the Royal Bank of Scotland). Three years later his career path took him to Uganda, as accountant at the Masaka Branch of National & Grindlays Bank, thus beginning a long association with Africa. In 1960 he moved to Kenya, managing sub-branches there until 1962 when he was appointed Manager of the Harambee Avenue Branch in Nairobi. Although his banking career formally ended in March 1964, he has since remained deeply concerned to maintain the highest professional and ethical standards in the industry. In 2005 he was elected an Honorary Fellow of the Institute of Bankers in Scotland, having been an associate member since 1957. This Honorary Fellowship was in recognition of his creating an award for professionalism and ethics in banking, the Hutton Gold Medal for Excellence, which is awarded annually by the Chartered Institute of Bankers in Scotland. In his *Foreword* to the Institute's publication of a new mandatory Professionalism and Ethics Course in 2008 there are two passages which sum up Bill Hutton's beliefs:

The ideal banker should embody professional competence and personal integrity, act with fairness and compassion, and thereby earn the trust and respect of those they serve. Ethical behaviour does not preclude earning high bonuses and salaries for the individual or good dividends for the shareholder, but it might set limits.

Primary professional and ethical responsibility for the good conduct of banks lies with their boards and management, but ethics is essentially a personal matter, so it is up to each individual to be guided by their own high standards. Ethical standards may surpass those set by law and regulation; and it may require some personal courage and conviction to strive for such higher standards.

Bill Hutton's second career was in the pharmaceutical industry. In April 1964 he joined the International Division of the large American company Pfizer, and held several posts in West Africa, particularly in Ghana, Liberia, Sierra Leone, and the Ivory Coast. In May 1966 he was appointed Pfizer's Regional Manager for West Africa, responsible for all operations in some 21 countries

Bill Hutton in Uganda

excluding Nigeria. In 1963 he obtained a Private Pilot's Licence to fly fixed wing aircraft, and later, in 1990, he went solo flying a helicopter.

In July 1970 Bill moved to another American pharmaceutical company, Abbott Laboratories, where he remained for nearly six years. He started as Regional Manager for Africa, responsible for operations in 40 African countries. In February 1973 he was promoted to Managing Director for Abbott Laboratories Ltd, UK. This division had annual domestic sales of $15 million, and export sales of $5 million. His final post with Abbott was as Regional Manager for Southern Europe, the Middle East and Africa, where he was responsible for all the activities of their Diagnostic Division, and formulated policies and plans for future development of that business.

Bill Hutton embarked on his final career in February 1976 as a self-employed business consultant through his wholly owned Kenya registered company, Finco Ltd, based in Nairobi. The company operated mainly in Kenya, advising on and implementing new businesses and investment projects here. The company also worked in the UK, Finland, Switzerland, The People's Republic of China, Sudan and Zimbabwe. Bill chose major clients of first-class standing who were willing and capable of promoting and delivering major projects to the developing world, comprising either services or equipment, or a package of both. One of his guiding principles was that 'good business had to be good business for all parties, including the supplier, the buyer, employees and local communities. Many major projects were concluded successfully, but there were some others which did not meet the required financial, technical and managerial standards for competence and integrity'.

Retiring in March 1995, Bill Hutton settled on the island of Guernsey, Channel Islands, living in a house built on the site of the former military camp of Fort George, which lies on the cliffs just to the south of St Peter Port. From his house there are superb views of the smaller islands of Sark, Brecqhou, Herm and Jethou.

However, the earlier purchase in June 1983 of Colwell Wood and Colwell Wood Cottage has been a project much closer to his heart. The search began by looking for a piece of ancient and mature broad-leaved woodland, which had a cottage, a stream and a pond. Colwell fulfilled all these criteria, although they came with a challenge: the cottage was derelict, with no mains services, the spring that supplied its water had been vandalised, it had no vehicular access and was further away from London than Bill would have wished. When he visited the Wood for the first time, however, he instantly appreciated the therapeutic sense of peace and agelessness which ancient woodland brings. The renovation of the Cottage and the exploration of the Wood's long and unexpectedly rich history became his most cherished projects. Bill lived here in the winter months of 1987/8 when he took a sabbatical to read Moral Philosophy and Psychology at Exeter University and, ever since, it has been a much loved retreat and bolthole, as well as being a sound investment.

There have been several other projects and campaigns during his retirement, particularly carrying out investigations into fraud on a *pro bono* basis. Bill Hutton developed methods of deterrence, detection and disruption with a view to encouraging review, redress and restitution in cases where wrongdoing was discovered. He investigated the questionable practices of an international investment management company which led to recompense for a friend being obtained from the investment managers. In 1997 he started an investigation into a case of the mis-selling of pensions by a major UK pension provider to a leading London hospital. When the evidence was presented against them an out-of-court payment of £100,000 was made to another friend, one of the victims by the pensions 'mis-selling'.

Alderney Breakwater

Bill Hutton's most important 'whistle-blowing' fraud investigation was carried out in Guernsey over an eight-year period between 1996 and 2004. The case revolved around the condition of the famous Victorian Breakwater for the main harbour of the island of Alderney, and whether the existing structure should be repaired and maintained, or whether a completely new breakwater was necessary. The decision was the responsibility of the Board of Administration of the States of Guernsey, since Alderney is part of the Bailiwick of Guernsey. The President of the Board of Administration strongly preferred the latter option, although the evidence from engineering surveys clearly showed that a new breakwater was not necessary and that maintaining the existing one was the most cost-effective option in the public interest. Bill Hutton and his associates discovered that advertisements inviting tenders for the construction of a new breakwater were published prematurely when this was clearly not appropriate: the evidence about the condition of the breakwater was either misrepresented to, or concealed from, the States of Guernsey. Furthermore, he suspected improper project selection and pre-solicitation bid-rigging in the proposed construction project, which could possibly cost the Guernsey tax-payer a capital sum of as much as £45 million.

Following his presentation of evidence to the Guernsey Deputies and the States government, the proposals for the refurbishment or replacement of the Breakwater were abandoned, the machinery of government was reformed in ways that should better protect and manage the island government's assets and project finances in future - and the Breakwater still stands there today (2016) intact, without any of the proposed capital expenditure having been required.

In 1992 Bill Hutton successfully petitioned the Court of the Lord Lyon for a grant of a coat of arms. Some of the elements in the armorial bearings illustrate his ancestry from the Leslie and Macdonald clans, while the two arrows represent the surname Hutton. The Swahili motto *Moja kwa moja*, means 'one by one', 'step by step', 'thoroughness' or 'get on with it' and the lion reflects his long association with Africa. The scales show his prevailing interest in truth, justice and fairness. However, the design can only illustrate a limited portion of Bill Hutton's diverse achievements, qualities and interests.

Bill's deep affection for the small secluded estate of Colwell Wood, with its ancient trees and prolific bluebells and wild flowers, cannot be easily incorporated into heraldry. From this affection arises a strong desire to preserve and protect this pristine woodland for the benefit and enjoyment of future generations. Equally, his achievements in the worlds of banking, commerce and industry cannot be represented adequately on a coat of arms.

Above all, his generosity, integrity, determination and sense of fair play have constantly been used to promote higher standards of conduct in all walks of life and have been employed for the public good rather than private gain.

William Leslie Hutton

INTRODUCTION

Colwell Wood Cottage, which today is a picturesque and secluded retreat, stands in a small clearing in the heart of Colwell Wood, just west of the village of Offwell in east Devon. Today it forms part of a woodland estate that includes Colwell Wood, Scrub Wood and part of Offwell Woods. This study traces the history of the estate or manor of Colwell from medieval times to 1725, and then the history of Colwell Wood and Colwell Wood Cottage to the present day.

Colwell Wood

As is often the case, the early history of the estate of Colwell is one of fragmentation and reconstruction, followed by further fragmentation, as families and their fortunes waxed and waned.

There is much history embedded in the smallest piece of English property, and Colwell, remote and rural then as now, was nevertheless caught up briefly in the Wars of the Roses, passing for a short time into the hands of the future King Richard III. A further brush with national history came about when the woods were purchased in the late 1790s by Admiral Sir Thomas Graves, who at the Battle of Copenhagen became a national hero.

Historically, the commercial value of the property was in its woodland, and timbers from Colwell Wood would have found their way into many locally built ships as well as buildings, including Offwell church roof.

It was during the ownership of Admiral Graves, and during the Napoleonic Wars, that Colwell Wood Cottage was built. The original purpose of the building remains uncertain: it might have been intended for the purpose that it eventually served, to house a gamekeeper or woodsman, but this usage came much later. We have speculated that it might have once been a sylvan retreat for Mary Graves, the Admiral's only child, who never married and spent most of her long life at Combe Raleigh. In the mid-nineteenth century it provided a modest dwelling for smallholders and at one point a butcher. After the death of Mary Graves in 1860 the building was probably neglected, and in 1874 the Cottage and associated land were sold out of the Graves family to the Marwood-Eltons of Widworthy Court. The property remained a part of the Widworthy estate until this was broken up and sold in the 1930s. During this era the cottage housed the gamekeepers and woodsmen employed by the Marwood-Eltons and their tenants, but after the break-up of the estate the cottage once again went into decline, and by the 1980s it was in a state of dereliction, until it was acquired and restored by the present owner.

Colwell Wood and Colwell Wood Cottage

The woods at Colwell, designated an Area of Outstanding Beauty, are the haunt of roe deer, foxes, badgers and a variety of birds and in spring they abound with native bluebells (*hyacinthoides non-scripta*), which cover some eighteen acres of the estate. These are considered environmental indicators of an ancient woodland.

Chapter One
MEDIEVAL COLWELL

The estate of Colwell lies in the parish of Offwell in east Devon, about two miles east of the town of Honiton. Although it was usually described as a manor, this term should be interpreted loosely, since there was no clearly identifiable manor house, nor were there apparently ever any tenants holding property by copyhold tenure, and there is no evidence that any manorial court was ever held in Colwell.

The earliest evidence

Our starting point is the Domesday Book, which was a remarkably detailed survey of every holding of land, compiled in 1086 on behalf of King William I; a contemporary chronicler remarked that the task was done so thoroughly that scarcely an ox, cow or pig escaped notice. Three names were usually mentioned for every property, these being the owner during the Saxon period before 1066; the landowner who held it directly from King William, who was known as the tenant-in-chief; and the sub-tenant to whom the tenant-in-chief had given a lease. The parish of Offwell contained three manors, of which Colwell was much the largest; the other two were Offwell itself and Smallicombe. The entry relating to Colwell (recorded as *Colewille* and *Colewilla*) reads:

> Rogo holds Colwell from Baldwin. Aelmer held it before 1066. It paid tax for 1 and a
> half hides.[1] Land for 8 ploughs. In the lordship 1 plough; 2 slaves; half hide.
> 6 villagers and 2 smallholders with one and half ploughs and 1 hide.
> Pasture: 300 acres; woodland: 80 acres; 5 cattle; 8 pigs; 57 sheep; 20 goats.
> Value: formerly 10 shillings, now 20 shillings.[2]

It will be seen that Colwell had 300 acres of pasture and 80 acres of woodland, and a diversity of livestock including 57 sheep, whereas Offwell manor comprised just over 100 acres and had only ten cattle. Colwell had land for eight ploughs and Offwell land for only two ploughs.

The Domesday Book is our first written evidence of the name Colwell and it has been suggested that the first element of the name might have originally referred to a river or brook named Coly, and that this was an old name for what is now known as Offwell Brook. The second element is from the Old English *wielle*, meaning 'spring'.[3] Alternatively, there might have been an occupant or owner named Cola or Colla.

---

[1] A hide in this context was approximately 120 acres; the term was used for tax assessment purposes.
[2] *Domesday Book, Volume 9: Devon*, edited Caroline Thorn and Agnes O'Driscoll (Phillimore: Chichester, 1985), Part One, page 108c).
[3] J E B Gover, A Mawer & F M Stenton, *The Place-Names of Devon* (Cambridge, 1932), part II, page 629. The place-name Culbeer, also in Offwell, appears in the Domesday Book as 'Collabera': the second element in this instance is from 'bearu', meaning 'wood'.

There appears to be no surviving record of the exact boundary of the manor of Colwell, but the settlement was undoubtedly concentrated in the southern part of the parish of Offwell, where there were farms called West Colwell (also known as 'Clappers Tenement') and Colwell Barton (also known as East Colwell), Colwell Mill and a small hamlet to the south of these called Colwell, which lies close to Offwell Brook and the border with the parish of Northleigh.

Colwell: 6 inch Ordnance Survey 1906 (surveyed 1903)[4]

---

[4] Reproduced by permission of the National Library of Scotland.

A 1658 seating plan for Offwell church[5] refers to Colwell House, which was then owned by the Collins family; this may represent what was once the manor house. It is possible to speculate that the ancient manor house stood on the site of the farmhouse now known as Dullimoor, which is within the hamlet of Colwell, but this is uncertain.

Standing somewhat apart from this area is Colwell Wood, which lies to the north-west of Colwell, on the western side of the parish of Offwell and almost due west of the church and village of Offwell. Colwell Wood may have formed a detached portion of the manor, separated by woodland areas called The Husk, Scrub Wood and Offwell Wood.

We know nothing about Aelmer, who held Colwell before 1066, nor do we know anything about the sub-tenant Rogo who was farming there in 1086. Within the manor, a portion of the land, called the 'lordship' or 'demesne', was reserved for the feudal overlord or tenant-in-chief, Baldwin. Baldwin was one of the most powerful and wealthy of William the Conqueror's 'robber barons', known variously as Baldwin the Sheriff, Baldwin of Exeter and Baldwin de Meulles (after his probable place of birth). He was the second son of Gilbert, count of Eu, who was descended illegitimately from Richard, first Duke of Normandy; his wife, Emma, was a kinswoman of the Conqueror. His estates were concentrated around Exeter and Okehampton, where he built a castle. His most recent biographer states: 'the fact that Baldwin's English estates were concentrated in the south-west, unlike those of many other of the greatest landholders, points to his having been most active at an early stage of the conquest, but not participating in the takeover of the midlands and the north ...'.[6]

A conglomerate of property known as the 'honour of Okehampton', which included the three Offwell manors, formed the core of Baldwin's massive territorial holding; in Devon he was granted in all 177 manors, comprising about 100,000 acres under cultivation, almost all of which were within the honour. Baldwin died shortly before 1 January 1091; it was reported by a chronicler that on this date a priest in Lisieux, Normandy, had a vision of several recently dead noblemen, and that Baldwin and his brother Richard were among these terrifying spectres who were in full armour.

The Courtenay family and the Honour of Okehampton

In the late twelfth century the honour of Okehampton came into the hands of the Courtenay family, who held it until 1461. The Courtenays were one of the greatest noble families of medieval England; they dominated the county of Devon as magnates and landowners (tenants-in-chief) to a much greater extent than most English counties were dominated by a single family. In 1293 Hugh de Courtenay inherited the earldom of Devon from his cousin, Isabel de Reviers (although he was not formally recognised as the earl until 1335), and the Courtenay family's influence and wealth grew throughout the fourteenth century. They were feudal overlords of Colwell by virtue of holding the honour of Okehampton directly from the Crown, but Colwell was a very small piece in a large jigsaw, and it is unlikely that the Courtenays took much personal interest in the manor; certainly we have

---

[5] Offwell Parish Registers, Devon Archives; see copy at page 27.
[6] Judith A Green, 'Baldwin [Baldwin de Meulles] (d.1086x90)', *Oxford Dictionary of National Biography*, (Oxford University Press, 2004). This is the best modern account of Baldwin.

no direct evidence that they ever stayed there or contributed to the history of Colwell. The identity of the honour of Okehampton tended to fade as the medieval period progressed, and by 1461 it was certainly no longer the distinct administrative unit that it had been in 1086.

The de Colwell family

After 1086 it seems likely that the descendants of Rogo retained an interest in Colwell, probably as the intermediate tenants. In the late twelfth or early thirteenth century, the de Colwell family emerged as the local tenants at Colwell, and names from both these families, de Rogo and de Colwell, can be found as witnesses to deeds and grants made to the small Augustinian priory of Canonsleigh in the parish of Burliscombe, which lies about 13 miles north-west of Colwell.[7]

In three separate grants made between 1195 and 1243, William de Colwell ('de Colewille'), with the consent of his wife Emma and his heirs, made over several small properties to help support the canons of Canonsleigh Priory. Among these transactions was the grant of 'common pasture wherever it lies throughout his land of Colewille', given at some point between 1195 and 1219, and the witnesses to this particular transfer included 'Simon son of Rogo', 'Roger son of Simon' and 'Gervase de Hoffawille'. At the same time, Simon de Rogo, as the feudal overlord of William de Colwell, made a deed confirming this earliest transaction, and again Gervase 'de Offewille' was one of the witnesses. The other properties donated by William and Emma de Colwell lay in the manor of Netherton, which lies just to the south of Colwell in the parish of Farway. Among the witnesses to one of these grants (made between about 1220 and 1230) were Gervase de Offwell ('Uffawille') and his son Stephen.[8]

William de Colwell was clearly a friend to the Augustinians at Canonsleigh, since he acted as a witness to their deeds on six occasions between about 1200 and 1243. Only one of these deeds can be dated precisely: in 1206 the Prior of Canonsleigh resolved a dispute with the Abbey of Quarr on the Isle of Wight concerning a conduit of water across land in Netherton. On two of these occasions, he signed the deed alongside his neighbour, Gervase de Offwell. Simon son of Rogo also acted as a witness to a Canonsleigh deed on one occasion at this period.

Partial remains of Canonsleigh Priory

---

[7] Canonsleigh was founded in about 1160 as a house for Augustinian canons. It was always a small and poorly endowed priory, and from about 1260 local gentry ceased giving it benefactions. In 1284, there were only seven canons remaining and their affairs were in some disorder. It was then re-established as a house for canonesses. Photograph by Derek Harper; licensed under a Creative Commons Generic Licence.

[8] This paragraph and the following ones relating to Canonsleigh are based on *The Cartulary of Canonleigh Abbey*, edited by Vera C M London (Devon & Cornwall Record Society, new series, vol 8, 1965, pages xxvii, 12–15, 56–67 and 101).

The survey of 1242/3 listed 'Willelmus de Colewell' as holding the fee[9] of Colwell from John de Courtenay without any reference to the de Rogo family.[10] From about 1230 onwards, the name Philip de Colwell appears as a witness to deeds and other documents relating to the Priory of Canonsleigh; in all, Philip witnessed eight separate documents in the period up to about 1250. He once signed his name alongside John de Colwell, but we can only guess as to how they were related to each other and to William and Emma. Ralph de Colwell undoubtedly represents a later generation of the family: in the year 1288 he witnessed two deeds for Canonsleigh, which was re-founded as a house for Augustinian canonesses shortly before this date. By these two deeds Nicholas de Mortesthorne conveyed to the canonesses the manor of Northleigh, which adjoins Colwell.

When the tax or aid of 1284–86 was levied, we find the manor of Colwell being held by 'Simon filius Rogonis (son of Rogo)'. His name also appears as a witness to a Canonsleigh deed dated 3 February 1286. However, it is unlikely that the de Rogo family lived at Colwell, whereas the successive generations using 'de Colwell' as a surname are likely to have lived there. The early seventeenth-century antiquary and historian Sir William Pole (died 1635) set out six generations of the de Colewell/de Colwill family:

> Colwell, in the parish of Offwell, hath had divers of that name inhabitants theire; namely, Henry de Colwill, Will(ia)m his sonne, Phillip, John, Thomas & Will(ia)m, w(hi)ch successively were lords thereof.[11]

Since Pole gives neither dates nor sources, his information is difficult to verify, but he may have been partially relying on the Canonsleigh cartulary.

Simon son of Rogo was still in possession of 'Colewille' when an inquisition post mortem was held at Exeter on Wednesday, St George's Day (23 April) 1292, into the property of Sir Hugh de Courtenay, the tenant-in-chief of the honour of Okehampton. At this point it was listed jointly with the manor of Holcombe Rogis ('Holecumbe'), which lies several miles to the north-west of Offwell, on the border with Somerset, and together they extended to five knights' fees, whereas Offwell was just one knight's fee.[12]

William and Genevieve de Park

Not long after 1292 there was a change of ownership. Sir William Pole reported:

> In Kinge Edw. tyme, about the latter end of his raigne, Walter Trenchard and Agnes his wief (w(hi)ch held Colwill in joynture after ye death of Raph Colwill) granted the grange of Colwill unto Will(ia)m de Park & Genouefa his wief.[13]

---

[9] In this context, a fee meant an estate.

[10] *Book of Fees commonly called Testa de Nevill*, part 2, page 785.

[11] Sir William Pole, *Collections towards a Description of the County of Devon* (London, 1791), page 146.

[12] A knight's fee was the area of land which enabled a knight to keep himself and his retinue, and to render his feudal services to his lord, for a year. *Calendar of Inquisitions Post Mortem*, vol 3, Edward I (HMSO, 1906), pages 23–29.

[13] Sir William Pole, *loc cit.*

Again, we are given no source for this information. The returns of the 1303 tax show that the joint owners of the manor of Colwell were William de Park and the Master of the Priory or Hospital of Bodmiscombe.[14] For the next 66 years (between 1303 and 1369) the main parts of the manors of Offwell and the manor of Colwell shared the same owners. In the following year, on 3 November 1304, we find a transaction by William de Park and his wife Genevieve in respect of Colwell, whereby their joint property was placed in the hands of William de Taunton, who then granted it back to William and Genevieve:

> At York, on the morrow of Souls, 3 November 1304
> Between William de Parco & Genovefa his wife (claimants) and William de Taunton (deforciant)
> Concerning: 1 messuage [dwelling], 1½ ploughlands, 10 acres of meadow, 30 acres of wood and 60 acres of pasture in Colewell.
> William and Genovefa acknowledged the property to be the right of William de Taunton as by their gift. For this William de Taunton granted the property to William and Genovefa and gave up the same to them at the court. To have and to hold to William and Genovefa and the heirs he shall have begotten on her, of the chief lords of that fee by the services which belong to the property for ever. Should William de Parco die without such heir, then after the deaths of both William and Genovefa the said property shall remain in its entirety to the right heirs of William. To hold of the chief lords of that fee by the services which belong to that property for ever.
> Henry son of Roger of Holcombe Rogus put in his claim.[15]

The area of woodland in Colwell was now 30 acres, whereas it had been 80 acres when the Domesday Book was compiled, but on the other hand we cannot be sure that William and Genevieve's holding included all the woodland in the manor. It will be seen that Henry son of Roger of Holcombe Rogus or Rogis, who was possibly the younger brother of Simon son of Roger, now registered his interest in Colwell. The fine shows that William and Genevieve held just 100 acres of land in Colwell, which is only about a quarter of the extent of the manor in the Domesday Book. It is of course possible that they had a larger holding, but only placed a portion of it in the hands of William de Taunton as a trustee.

The de Courtenay family in the fourteenth century

In May 1311 another fine shows that William and Genevieve de Park granted their property in Colwell and Holcombe Rogis to Philip de Courtenay, but Philip then granted them back a life interest in the property.[16] Philip cannot be identified with certainty, but he was possibly a younger brother of Sir Hugh de Courtenay of Okehampton who died in 1291:

---

[14] *Feudal Aids, 1284–1431*, page 366 ('Willelmus de Park et Magister Hospitalis de Bothemiscomb').

[15] *Devon Feet of Fines*, vol 2: 1272–1369, No 906. These record the judgements as to the ownership of land and property, being often the result of a collusive action to establish title. The judgement itself was the 'fine' (from the Latin *finis*, meaning 'end').

[16] This transaction was broadly similar to the one they made 30 years later in respect of Offwell with Thomas de Courtenay.

> At Westminster, 3 weeks from Easter day, 2 May 1311
> Between *Philip de Curtenay* (Claimant) and *William de Parco & Genovefa his wife*
> (Deforciants)
> Concerning: 1 messuage, 2 ploughlands, 17 acres of meadow, 100 acres of pasture, 60
> acres of wood and 9 pence of rent in Colewell and Combe
> William acknowledged the tenements to be the right of Philip as by William's gift. For this
> Philip granted the tenements to William and Genovefa and gave them up to them at the Court.
> To have and to hold to William and Genovefa during their lives of Philip and his heirs.
> Rendering therefor yearly one rose at the feast of the Nativity of St John Baptist (24 June) for
> all service, custom and exaction to the said Philip and his heirs belonging, and rendering
> therefore to the chief lords of that fee on behalf of Philip and his heirs all other services which
> to those tenements belong. After the deaths of William and Genevefa the tenements shall revert
> in their entirety to Philip and his heirs, quit of the heirs of William and Genovefa. To hold of
> the chief lords of that fee by the services which to those tenements belong for ever
> Ralph de Colwell put in his claim
> Henry Rogis, son of Simon Rogis, put in his claim.[17]

Philip de Courtenay's interest in Colwell and Holcombe Rogis was fairly nominal, since William and Genevieve were both relatively young in 1311, and perhaps they wished to raise money secured on their property in a similar fashion to a modern mortgage. It will be seen that Ralph de Colwell and Henry, son of Simon Rogis, registered their interests in Colwell and Holcombe Rogis, which indicates that William and Genevieve possessed only part of both manors. In 1311 the size of William and Genevieve's holding appears to have increased considerably since 1304; they now held 177 acres including 60 acres of woodland, but we are not told what proportion of this land lay in Holcombe Rogis.

We have no evidence as to what became of Philip de Courtenay's contingent interest, or remainder, in Colwell; he may have sold it to his kinsman Sir Thomas de Courtenay, or Sir Thomas may have acquired it by inheritance. In any event the tax return of 1346 showed that Thomas de Courtenay was now in possession of nine tenths of Colwell, and the master of the Hospital of Bodmiscombe owned a twentieth part:

> De Thomas de Courtenay pro decima nona parte un f(eodum) m(ilitis) in Colwill tentam
> de honore de Holcombe Regis (*sic*), quam Willelmus de Parco quondam tenuit:
> 2 shillings 1 pence (tax).
> (*Of Thomas de Courtenay for a nine-tenths part of a knight's fee in Colwill held of the honour of Holcombe Regis, which William de Parco once held.*)
>
> De magistro Hospitular tenet vicesimam partem un f(eodum) m(ilitis) in Colwyll tentam de
> honore de Holecomb Regis in capite in puram et perpetuam elemosinam
> (*Of the Master of the Hospitallers for a twentieth part of a knight's fee in Colwell held of the honour of Holcombe Regis in chief as a charitable gift.*)[18]

---

[17] *Devon Feet of Fines*, vol 2: 1272–1369, no 975.
[18] *Feudal Aids* 1284–1431, page 428.

This confirms that William and Genevieve de Park were now dead, and the entries are very similar to those for Offwell in the same tax return. However, somewhat surprisingly, Colwell was described as being in the honour of Holcombe Rogis.

Sir Thomas de Courtenay died in June 1362, and two inquisitions post mortem were carried out on his estates in Devon, on 29 September 1362 and 14 January 1363. The first of these reported that 'long before his death' Sir Thomas had placed the manor of Sutton Lucy and Colwell ('Colewylle'), together with several other properties in Devon, in the hands of three trustees, these being his elder brother, Hugh de Courtenay, Earl of Devon, his son-in-law Sir John Dinham (died 1383) and Roger Torell. The purpose of the trust was not disclosed. 'Sutton Lucy' almost certainly refers to Sutton Barton, which lies just to the east of Colwell in the parish of Widworthy; it would appear that for administrative convenience these two manors were united by Sir Thomas de Courtenay. The inquisition also reported that Sutton Lucy and Colwell were both held 'in chief' by Hugh de Courtenay, Earl of Devon. The second inquisition merely reported that Sutton Lucy and Colwell were two of six manors in Devon that Sir Thomas held from his feudal superior and brother, the Earl of Devon.

Since Sir Thomas's only son and heir, Hugh de Courtenay, was aged twelve when his father died, the boy was made a ward of the Crown, which meant that his estates were administered by the Crown's officer in Devon, known as the escheator, and the Crown became responsible for his upbringing and marriage. The Crown frequently used lands held in wardship to support members of the royal family or to reward loyal service. In this case, the revenues from Sir Thomas de Courtenay's estates were granted to King Edward III's eldest daughter, Isabella of Woodstock (born 1332, died 1379), who was married to Enguerrand de Courcy, Earl of Bedford. Thus the rents and income from Colwell would have been delivered to Princess Isabella during the period 1362 to 1369. Hugh de Courtenay died on 12 August 1369, which was about a couple of years before he reached his majority, and thus another series of inquisitions post mortem was carried out on his estates, which were still in the hands of the Crown. The inquisition taken at Exeter on 26 September 1369 showed that Hugh held the following manor:

> Sutton Lucy and Colewill: a messuage and 2 carucates[19] of land, held of the Earl of Devon by service of a fourth part of a knight's fee, and pleas and perquisites of court worth 40 pence yearly.

This brief description suggests that Hugh de Courtenay's property in Colwell was somewhat smaller than that owned by William and Genevieve de Park there in 1311.

Hugh de Courtenay had two sisters, the elder of whom was Muriel who married Sir John Dinham; their son John Dinham was allocated Offwell. The younger sister was Margaret who was aged seventeen (or seventeen and a half) when the inquisitions post mortem were carried out in the autumn of 1369. After the death of her parents (Thomas and Muriel de Courtenay) the Crown appointed John Hill and William Tannere to act as guardians to Margaret.[20] On 27 November 1369, the King, having obtained the consent of Princess Isabella and the two guardians, ordered the

---

[19] A carucate was equivalent to a hide.
[20] *Calendar of Fine Rolls, 1369–1377*, page 45.

'purparty' (portion) of the manor of Sutton Lucy with Colwell (*recte Colewyl*) to be handed over to Margaret, she now being aged 'seventeen and more'. This division of Hugh de Courtenay's estates between his two sisters was made by the Court of Chancery in London. It was almost certainly made in anticipation of Margaret's marriage to Thomas Peverell.

The Peverell family

The Peverells were a relatively minor local gentry family, whose main manors in Devon were Whelmstone, in the parish of Colebrooke, and Sampford Peverell, which lies to the north west of Offwell, close to Holcombe Rogis. They also held several manors in Cornwall, such as Parke, Hamatethy and Penhale. Thomas Peverell appears to have played no part in local administration, nor did he hold any important public office. The marriage would have been seen as a good one, partly because his bride was a granddaughter of the Earl of Devon, and partly because by their marriage she brought several valuable properties in Devon into his hands. Among these were Pool, Plymtree and Harleston, whereas Sutton Lucy and Colwell were probably among the less valuable additions to the Peverell family estates. As always, the Crown was able to make a charge for drawing up the partition of Hugh de Courtenay's estates between his sisters. In Margaret's case she was charged 100 shillings, but payment was delayed until Easter 1383, when she and Thomas Peverell appeared at the Court of the Exchequer in London, where they gave homage for the properties.[21]

An inquisition post mortem on the estate of his feudal overlord, Hugh de Courtenay, Earl of Devon, confirms that Thomas Peverell (in right of his wife) held Colwell in August 1377.[22]

Margaret Peverell died on 14 August 1422, and inquisitions post mortem were carried out on her estates in Devon, Somerset and Cornwall. The jurors on the inquisition into her property in Devon, who met at Exeter on 8 December 1422, gave the following interesting report on her property at Colwell:

> Long before her death she (Margaret Peverell) granted a messuage and a carucate in Colwill to John Dennyng who survives, Joan his late wife and Joan their daughter deceased, for their lives, rendering to Margaret and her heirs 50 shillings at Christmas, Easter, Midsummer and Michaelmas in equal portions. Afterwards, by her indented deed shown to the jurors, she granted the rent and services to John, Joan and Joan, with reversion of the lands and tenements, to Nicholas Bokelly, who survives, for life, rendering to Margaret and her heirs a grain of wheat. She died seised of this grain and the reversion. The messuage and carucate are held of the heirs of Hugh Courtenay, late earl of Devon, in the King's wardship.[23]

Thus, 'long before her death' in August 1422, Margaret Peverell had granted a lease of about half the land in her manor of Colwell to John Dennyng, his wife and his daughter (who were both called

---

[21] 'Extract from Exchequer Memoranda Roll, Easter Term 1383' (copy of document in Arundell papers: Cornwall Record Office AR1/912: Devon and Somerset).

[22] *Calendar of Inquisitions Post Mortem*, vol 14 (Edward III), page 14.

[23] *Calendar of Inquisitions Post Mortem*, vol 22 (1422–1427). The editor of the *Calendar* identifies Colwell as 'Colwill' in the parish of Egg Buckland, just outside Plymouth, but this is almost certainly an error.

Joan) for the duration of their lives. The Dennyng family was charged an annual rent of 50 shillings, paid quarterly. By a later deed, it was agreed that after the death of the longest survivor of these three members of the Dennyng family, the property was to pass to Nicholas Bokelly, for the duration of his life. In December 1422 John Dennyng was still living, but his wife and daughter were dead. Nicholas Bokelly was still alive; he paid Margaret a nominal rent of one grain of wheat. We have traced no further information about the Dennyng family or Nicholas Bokelly, but it seems likely that they were local farmers living in Colwell in the early fifteenth century; and it would have been they who tilled the land there. Thus we get a rare glimpse of the ordinary inhabitants of Colwell in the middle ages.

In the same year, Margaret's feudal overlord, Hugh Courtenay, Earl of Devon, also died (on 16 June 1422). The jurors gave very out-of-date information about Colwell Barton, referring apparently to Colwell as a whole, reporting that the sub-tenants were 'the heirs of William de Parco' and the Master of the Priory or Hospital of Bodmiscombe, and that it was worth 100 shillings. The earl's widow, Anne, dowager countess of Devon, was given her dowager's interest and one of the properties assigned to her in February 1423 was 'half a knight's fee in Colewille sometime held by the heir of William de Parco and the Master of Batheneyscombe (Bodmiscombe)'.

We do not know precisely when Thomas Peverell died, but as happened so frequently in the history of both Offwell and Colwell, there was failure of male heirs; he and Margaret had only two daughters, and so once again there must have been a partition of his property, which would have included Colwell. According to the inquisitions held on her mother's estates, the elder daughter, Eleanor Peverell, was born in about 1381/2. She married twice, first to Otto Trenewith, who was dead by August 1422, and secondly to Sir William Talbot, who was her husband in December of that year. Eleanor had no children by either husband, and she died on 11 April 1439. The younger daughter was Katherine Peverell; she was probably born shortly before 1393[24] and at a very young age she married Sir Walter Hungerford, later first Lord Hungerford.

The Hungerford family and Richard III

The marriage of Katherine Peverell to Sir Walter Hungerford was arranged by Walter's father as early as 1396, and it possibly took place before May 1399; they were certainly married by 18 September 1402, when the Pope granted the couple permission to use a portable altar for saying mass. This marriage was a very advantageous one, since Sir Walter Hungerford was an extremely successful soldier, politician and diplomat and a tireless supporter of the Lancastrian dynasty. He distinguished himself at the battle of Agincourt (1415) and among the many high offices he held were Speaker of the House of Commons (1414) and Treasurer of England (1426–1432).

Katherine Hungerford died young; we do not know precisely when, but she was still living on 14 June 1426 when her husband was granted a licence to found a perpetual chantry chapel in his parish

---

[24] She was aged '28 and more' in December 1422 according to her mother's inquisition post mortem, but in view of the date of her marriage, this was probably an underestimate (*History of Parliament: House of Commons 1386–1421, vol 3* (Stroud, 1993), sub 'Sir Walter Hungerford' and 'Sir William Talbot', *Complete Peerage* sub 'Hungerford').

church of Farleigh Hungerford, Somerset, since he requested that prayers be said for her soul there after her death. She predeceased her sister Eleanor, who died in 1439; by this date Walter Hungerford had remarried to Eleanor, Countess of Arundel, the widow of John, Earl of Arundel (died 1421). We know that Katherine was buried in Salisbury Cathedral, since Walter requested to be buried there alongside her.

We do not know which of the two Peverell sisters (Eleanor or Katherine) was allocated Colwell after the death of their mother in 1422, but on Eleanor's death in 1439 the manor would have passed into the hands of either Sir Walter himself (by right of his widow) or to his son and heir, Robert Hungerford, as heir to his aunt Eleanor (Peverell) Talbot.

Walter, first Lord Hungerford, died on 9 August 1449; he had grown extremely wealthy and held property in Devon, Cornwall, Middlesex, Somerset, Dorset, Oxfordshire, Hampshire, Berkshire and Wiltshire. His heir was his eldest son (by Katherine Peverell), Robert, second Lord Hungerford, who thus became the next owner of Colwell. On the death of his aunt Eleanor (Peverell) Talbot in 1439, Robert's age was given as 26, but in fact he was probably a few years older.

The second Lord Hungerford played little part in public life, but his affection for his mother was shown in his will, in which he bequeathed 25 marks for the repair of a highway which his father had

built 'for the health of the soul of Katherine, his late consort'.[25] The second Lord Hungerford died on 18 May 1459 and was buried in Salisbury Cathedral; his son and heir, also named Robert, became the third Lord Hungerford. Born shortly before 1429, he spent about six years as a prisoner of war in France, following the English defeat in Gascony in 1453. On his return to England, the outbreak of the Wars of the Roses meant that he immediately saw military action again, on the Lancastrian side. When the Yorkists triumphed in March 1461, he was attainted and his estates were forfeited. The new King (Edward IV) granted Hungerford's estates to his brother Richard, Duke of Gloucester, and thus Colwell was briefly in the hands of the future King Richard III. Meanwhile, Hungerford joined the Lancastrian army in Scotland, which invaded England in the spring of 1464. This Lancastrian army was defeated at the battle of Hexham, Northumberland; Hungerford was captured after the battle and beheaded at Newcastle on 18 May 1464.

Richard III, by unknown artist. Oil on panel, late 16ᵗʰ century[26]

---

[25] *Complete Peerage* sub 'Hungerford'.
[26] © National Portrait Gallery, London: NPG 148.

Robert's son and heir was Sir Thomas Hungerford, and King Edward went to some lengths to attempt to reconcile him to the Yorkist regime. He escaped attainder and was pardoned in November 1462, and was even knighted by the King, despite the fact that his father was an active rebel. Only three weeks before Robert was executed, the King returned the manors of Sutton Lucy, Colwell and Whelmstone to Sir Thomas Hungerford and his wife:

> 23 Apr 1464: Commitment to Sir Thomas Hungerford Kt., and his wife Anne ... of the keeping of manors of Sutton Lucy, Colewill and Wolmeston (Whelmstone), Devon, which have been taken into the King's hands by an Inquisition, to hold until Easter next, they to answer at the Exchequer for issues taken from it.[27]

Thus we may claim that Colwell played a small part in national politics during the turbulent Wars of the Roses. In reality, the offer of these three manors was not very generous and was only for the duration of a year; they would not have yielded a great deal of income. The most valuable of the three was Whelmstone in the parish of Colebrooke, near Crediton, which was the main manor of Hungerford's great-great-grandfather, Thomas Peverell.

Sir Thomas Hungerford was never fully reconciled to the Yorkist regime; he was a close ally and friend of his feudal overlord, Henry Courtenay (who was the rightful earl of Devon). King Edward IV similarly tried to woo Courtenay into the Yorkist fold by allowing him a generous share of the forfeited estates of his late brother, the Earl of Devon, who was killed in 1461. Although neither Hungerford nor Courtenay showed any inclination to support the Yorkists, they were allowed to live quietly on their estates until, in November 1468, they were arrested in Wiltshire and imprisoned at Salisbury. They were brought before a special commission headed by Richard, Duke of Gloucester, and charged with treason; it was asserted that on 21 May 1468 and on other occasions they had plotted with the exiled Lancastrian Queen Margaret of Anjou to bring about 'the final death and final destruction of the Most Christian Prince, Edward IV'. It was a trumped-up charge based on unconvincing evidence, but a jury of 16 men found them guilty, and the King himself came to Salisbury to witness their downfall. On 17 January 1469 'they were subjected to the fullest and protracted horrors of a fifteenth-century political execution': they were hung, drawn and quartered at Bemerton, just outside Salisbury.[28]

The fate of Colwell after the execution of Sir Thomas Hungerford has not been established; it was possibly returned to Richard, Duke of Gloucester, who had played a vindictive role in Hungerford's downfall. Sir Thomas's heir was his two-year-old daughter, Mary; she may have regained her rightful inheritance for a brief period in late 1470 and early 1471 when the Lancastrian dynasty, under King Henry VI, was restored for six months, but the family had to wait until Henry Tudor won the throne in August 1485 before the attainders of 1461 were fully reversed. In 1481 Mary Hungerford married Edward, Lord Hastings. Their son and heir, George Hastings, was born in about 1488 and was created earl of Huntingdon in 1529. Thus the manor of Colwell once again passed through the female line, into the ownership of the earls of Huntingdon.

---

[27] *Calendar of Fine Rolls* 1461–1471, page 133.
[28] Charles Ross, *Edward IV* (London, 1974), page 123.

Chapter Two
EARLY MODERN HISTORY

We do not know exactly when the earls of Huntingdon sold the manor of Colwell, but according to Polwhele's *History of Devonshire* it was sold by 'Henry, Earl of Huntingdon, unto William Franklin'.[29] Polwhele gives no date for the transaction, but he was presumably referring to Henry Hastings, who succeeded his father as the 19th earl in June 1560, and who died in December 1595. In an article in the *Western Morning News* of 17 March 1950, Colonel J Ramsden claimed that the Franklin family of Widworthy and Colwell were probably related to the eighteenth-century American statesman, Benjamin Franklin. He offered no precise evidence for this but pointed out that the parish registers of Widworthy showed five members of the Franklin family with the given name Benjamin between 1618 and 1682. From about 1700 onwards the surname Franklin gradually disappeared from the Widworthy registers, prompting speculation that they migrated to America. The Franklins sold Colwell in about 1614, and so they held it for 50 years or less.

The Collins family

William Collins, who was baptised on 5 February 1565 in Offwell, bought the manor of Colwell from his brother-in-law Peter Franklin of Widworthy, and five other members of the Franklin family, probably in or very shortly after 1614. The evidence for this sale comes from an undated draft document of agreement for 'remise and quitclaim',[30] written in heavily abbreviated Latin, which is held at the Devon Archives in the Marwood Elton Collection.[31] The draft can be briefly summarised:

> (1) Oliver Franckelyn gent, Peter Franckelyn gent, John Franckelyn, Benjamin Franckelyn, Samuel Franckelyn and Jeremy Cheriton and Anne his wife
> (2) William Collens gent of the manor of Colwell
> (1) conveys to (2):
> Manor of Colwell with appurtenances, with five messuages, two mills, eight gardens, 200 acres of land, 50 acres of meadow, 100 acres of pasture, 50 acres of wood and 400 acres of furze and heath, with appurtenances in Offwell, and one quarry, with appurtenances, in Sutton Lucy and Widworthy.[32]

The Devon Archives catalogue, probably following the opinion of Colonel Ramsden, dates the document as 'circa 1590s' but this is almost certainly at least 25 years too early since it mentions

---

[29] Polwhele, *History of Devonshire*, (1793–1806), vol 2, page 321.

[30] A 'remise' was a transfer of property; a 'quitclaim' was the formal renunciation of interest in the property by the vendors following the sale.

[31] Devon Archives: Marwood Elton Collection, 281M/T4.

[32] Several phrases have been inserted and then crossed out at the end of this section.

Jeremy Cheriton and his wife Ann: Ann(e) Franklin married Jeremy Cheriton on 27 September 1614 at Widworthy,[33] and so the deed must have been drawn up after this date, or possibly in anticipation of the marriage.

This draft deed does not reveal how the joint vendors of the manor of Colwell and the quarry in Sutton Lucy and Widworthy were related to each other, but we are reasonably certain that Oliver Franklin, who was named first, was the father of Peter, John, Benjamin, Samuel and Anne who was the wife of Jeremy Cheriton. We find support for this in a lease, dated 30 October 1590, by which Oliver Franklin, gentleman of Buckfastleigh, Devon, and his son Peter, granted a property defined as 'a messuage called Come in Offwell, part of the manor of Sutton Lucy and Colwell' to Thomas Marwood of Northleigh for the period of 60 years.[34]

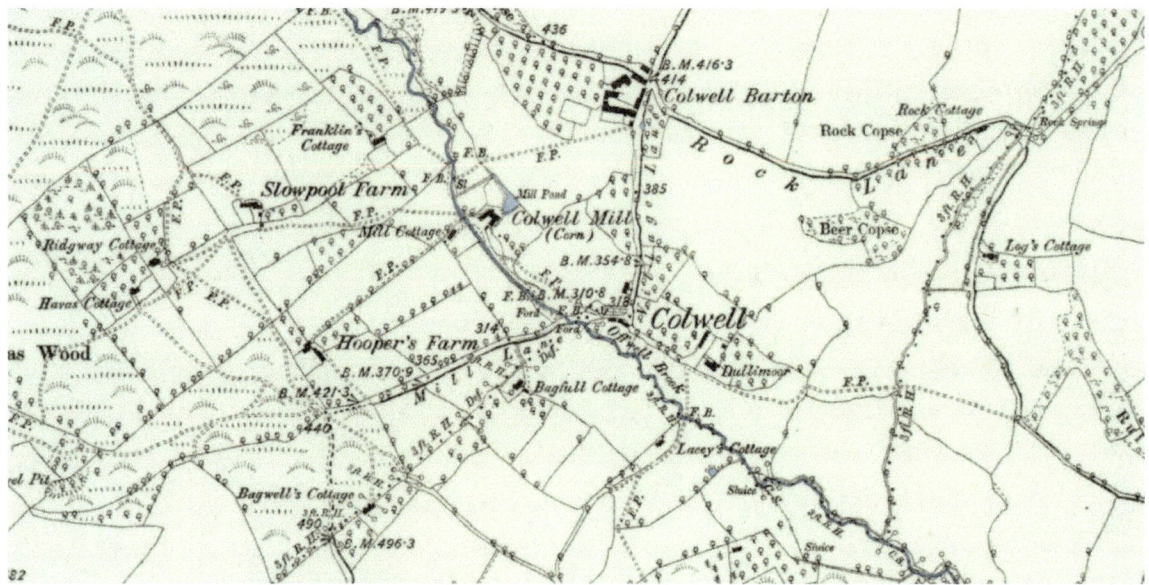

Colwell Mill: 6 inch Ordnance Survey 1889 (surveyed 1888)[35]

The draft deed indicates that there were two mills in Colwell in about 1614. One of these was identified by Colonel J Ramsden in his *Parochial History of Offwell and Widworthy, Honiton* (1946) as the 'ancient mill' situated in Husk Copse between Colwell and Offwell Woods, just to the south west of the lower of the two fish ponds there. There appears to be no documentary evidence of this mill, which was not marked on any maps; Ramsden believed it had been abandoned by 1789, and (writing in 1946) added:

---

[33] *International Genealogical Index.*

[34] Devon Archives 281M/T3 (from catalogue only). On 21 January 1599 Thomas Marwood assigned the lease to his son, Thomas Marwood junior, and on 20 May 1608, the lease was again assigned to a third generation called Thomas Marwood of Northleigh: Devon Archives 281M/T5.

35 Devonshire LXXI.NW. Reproduced by permission of the National Library of Scotland.

No trace of the Mill can now be seen but the site of its wheel pit is very obvious. It was fed by a leat, which can be traced from the spring below Colwell House[36] and by another bringing water from the springs in Colwell Wood. The site is only 100 yards east of the lane from Honiton to Colyton, which must have been a busy pack horse track and trade route for trade proceeding to the harbour near Axmouth.[37]

The main mill in Colwell was on the east bank of Offwell Brook, just to the south west of Colwell Barton farm, and to the north of Mill Lane. This is clearly marked as 'Colwell Mill (corn)' on the 1888/9 Ordnance Survey map; adjoining the mill was a Mill Pond and Mill Cottage. According to Ramsden, this mill was in constant use until it was burnt down in about 1890; it was no longer marked on the 1906 Ordnance Survey map (surveyed in 1903).

The Collins family had been settled in Colwell for at least half a century before William purchased the manor from the Franklin family; his baptism in February 1565 was the first occasion on which the surname was recorded in the parish registers (which commence in 1551). William's father, Thomas Collins, was described as a yeoman of Colwell in a deed dated 31 October 1566.[38] Six years later, in July 1573, Thomas Collins, who was again described as a yeoman, and his son William, purchased the substantial property of West Colwell from John Lowman (who in turn had purchased it from Richard Mallett esquire):

> Bargain and sale by John Lowman of Farwaye, gentleman, to Thomas Collyns, yeoman, and William Collyns his son, of the messuages, farms, lands, pastures, commons, woods, rents etc, in West Colwell in Offwell, in the tenure of Johanne Clappe widow, called West Colwell, which he purchased of Richard Mallett esq., as appears by a deed indented 10 September last.[39]

This deed shows that by 1573 West Colwell, which was also known as 'Clappers Tenement', no doubt after the Clappe family who were tenants there over a long period, had become detached from the manor of Colwell. The 1573 deed made no mention of the Franklin family's ownership of the manor and thus it would seem likely that West Colwell was detached and sold to Richard Mallett by the Hastings family (earls of Huntingdon) at some point in the first half of the sixteenth century. West Colwell was to become the principal home of the Collins family. The name 'Mr Collins' features twice in the parish rate list of 1578, one of these men being 'of Williamton'; and the first signatory to this list was Thomas Collins.

When the King's heralds made their visitation of Devon in about 1620,[40] recording pedigrees of the gentry and making sure that coats of arms were being legitimately used, they noted that Thomas Collyns (son of Thomas and Sibell Collyns of Ottery or 'Awtrie' St Mary) married Joane, daughter

---

[36] This presumably refers to the modern Colwell House.
[37] Colonel J Ramsden, *Parochial History* (1946), chapter 5.
[38] John C Tingey, 'Calendar of Deeds Enrolled within the County of Devon' (typed abstracts, Devon Archives), no 777.
[39] *Ibid*, No 988.
[40] Frederick Thomas Colby, ed, *The Publications of the Harleian Society, volume 6: The Visitation of the County of Devon in the Year 1620* (London, England: Taylor and Co, 1872), pages 67–68.

THE COLLINS FAMILY

Owners of Colwell are underlined

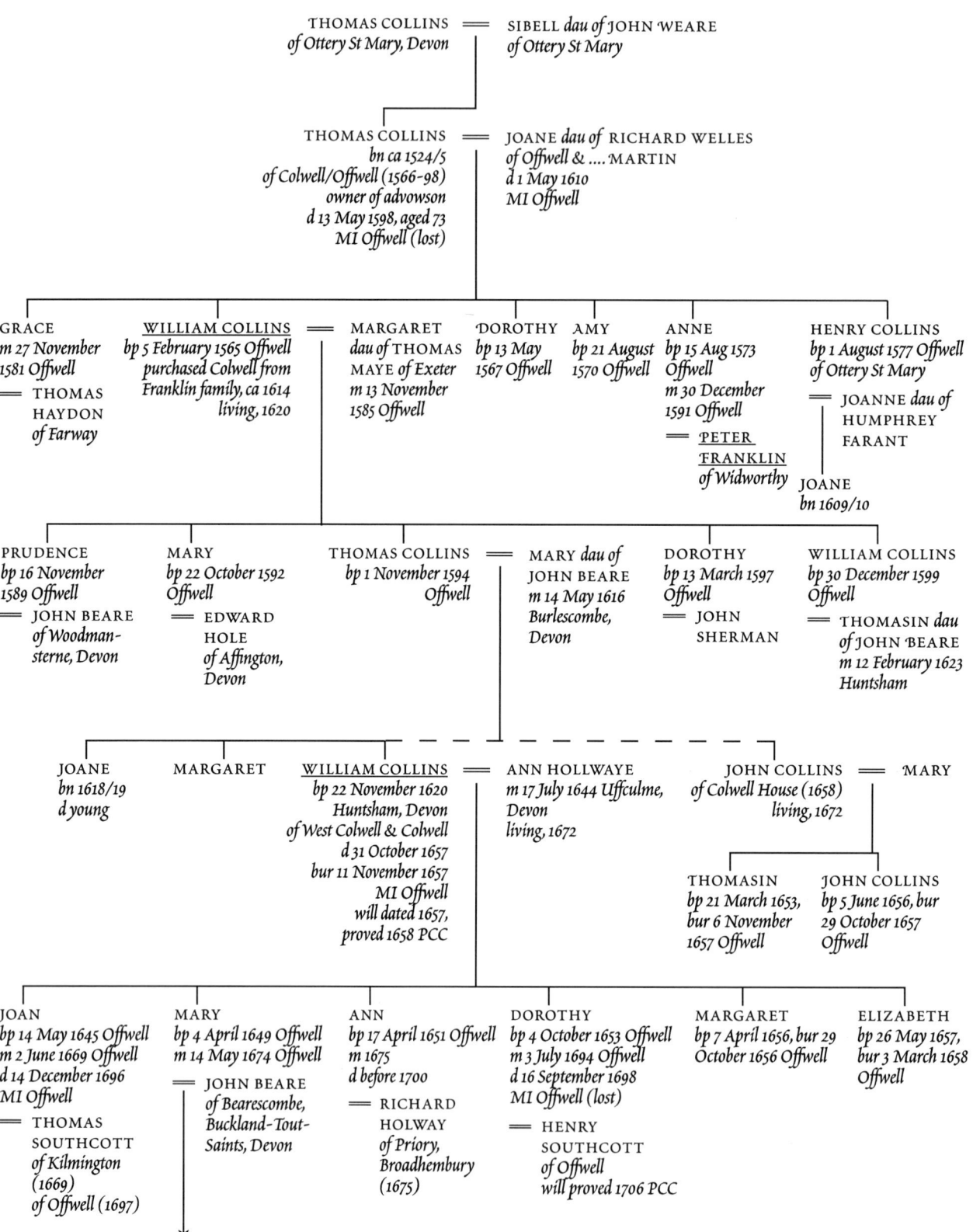

THOMAS COLLINS == SIBELL *dau of* JOHN WEARE
of Ottery St Mary, Devon *of Ottery St Mary*

THOMAS COLLINS == JOANE *dau of* RICHARD WELLES
bn ca 1524/5 *of Offwell & .... MARTIN*
of Colwell/Offwell (1566-98) *d 1 May 1610*
owner of advowson *MI Offwell*
d 13 May 1598, aged 73
MI Offwell (lost)

GRACE
m 27 November
1581 Offwell
== THOMAS
HAYDON
of Farway

WILLIAM COLLINS == MARGARET
bp 5 February 1565 Offwell *dau of* THOMAS
purchased Colwell from MAYE *of Exeter*
Franklin family, ca 1614 *m 13 November*
living, 1620 *1585 Offwell*

DOROTHY
bp 13 May
1567 Offwell

AMY
bp 21 August
1570 Offwell

ANNE
bp 15 Aug 1573
Offwell
m 30 December
1591 Offwell
== PETER
FRANKLIN
of Widworthy

HENRY COLLINS
bp 1 August 1577 Offwell
of Ottery St Mary
== JOANNE *dau of*
HUMPHREY
FARANT

JOANE
bn 1609/10

PRUDENCE
bp 16 November
1589 Offwell
== JOHN BEARE
of Woodman-
sterne, Devon

MARY
bp 22 October 1592
Offwell
== EDWARD
HOLE
of Affington,
Devon

THOMAS COLLINS == MARY *dau of*
bp 1 November 1594 JOHN BEARE
Offwell *m 14 May 1616*
Burlescombe,
Devon

DOROTHY
bp 13 March 1597
Offwell
== JOHN
SHERMAN

WILLIAM COLLINS
bp 30 December 1599
Offwell
== THOMASIN *dau*
of JOHN BEARE
m 12 February 1623
Huntsham

JOANE
bn 1618/19
d young

MARGARET

WILLIAM COLLINS == ANN HOLLWAYE
bp 22 November 1620 *m 17 July 1644 Uffculme,*
Huntsham, Devon *Devon*
of West Colwell & Colwell *living, 1672*
d 31 October 1657
bur 11 November 1657
MI Offwell
will dated 1657,
proved 1658 PCC

JOHN COLLINS == MARY
of Colwell House (1658) *living, 1672*

THOMASIN
bp 21 March 1653,
bur 6 November
1657 Offwell

JOHN COLLINS
bp 5 June 1656, bur
29 October 1657
Offwell

JOAN
bp 14 May 1645 Offwell
m 2 June 1669 Offwell
d 14 December 1696
MI Offwell
== THOMAS
SOUTHCOTT
of Kilmington
(1669)
of Offwell (1697)

MARY
bp 4 April 1649 Offwell
m 14 May 1674 Offwell
== JOHN BEARE
of Bearescombe,
Buckland-Tout-
Saints, Devon

ANN
bp 17 April 1651 Offwell
m 1675
d before 1700
== RICHARD
HOLWAY
of Priory,
Broadhembury
(1675)

DOROTHY
bp 4 October 1653 Offwell
m 3 July 1694 Offwell
d 16 September 1698
MI Offwell (lost)
== HENRY
SOUTHCOTT
of Offwell
will proved 1706 PCC

MARGARET
bp 7 April 1656, bur 29
October 1656 Offwell

ELIZABETH
bp 26 May 1657,
bur 3 March 1658
Offwell

and sole heiress of Richard Welles of Offwell, and thus it may have been through marriage into the Well(e)s family that the Collins family first acquired property in Offwell. Richard Welles' wife was the daughter of 'Martin of Offwell'. We have no date for the Collins/Welles marriage, but it was probably in the 1560s, and the visitation pedigree indicates that they had two sons and two daughters (see our pedigree chart on page 24).

Clearly, during the second half of the sixteenth century, the Collins family were actively acquiring property in Colwell and Offwell, by purchase and perhaps also by marriage. Thus during the period from about 1573 until 1657, the previously fragmented portions of the manor of Colwell were gradually reunited into the ownership of the one family.

Thomas and Joan's second son, William Collins, the purchaser of the manor of Colwell, married at Offwell in 1585, as the following entry in the parish register shows:

> 13 Nov 1585   Wills Collyns filius [son of] Thome Collyns de Colwill, et Margareta
> Maye filia [daughter of] Thome Maye de Exon [of Exeter] [married]

This confirms that Thomas Collins was living in Colwell several years before his son William purchased the manor. This is supported by a memorial in Offwell church, now lost, to Thomas Collins 'in his 74th year', which read:

> *THOMAS COLLYNS OF OFFWELL AND PATRON OF THIS CHURCH*
> *WHO DECEASED THE 13 DAIE OF MAY ANNO DOMINI 1598 AET SUAE 74*[41]

An undated list of charitable benefactions to the parish of Offwell, probably drawn up in about 1620, shows that 'Thomas Collins gent.' had given £6 8s 4d to the poor of the parish. His widow, Joan Collins, died in 1610 and her memorial has survived in a floor slab in Offwell church:

> *HERE LIETH THE BODIE OF JOHAN COLLYNS*
> *THE WIFE OF THOMAS COLLYNS GENT WHO*
> *DIED THE 1 DAY OF MAY ANNO DNI 1610*

The memorial was probably made later than 1610, since it is incorporated with that of Joan's descendant William Collins who died in 1657. It lies beneath the arch that divides the chancel from the north aisle and marks the entrance to the Collins vault; the family used the east end of the north aisle effectively as a private chapel. The parish registers of Offwell show that Thomas and Joan's younger daughter Anne married Peter Franklin in December 1591:

> 30 Dec 1591   Petrus [Peter] Francklin et Anna Collyns nupti fuereunt [married]

---

[41] *Devon & Cornwall Notes & Queries*, vol 6, page 298, cited by Ramsden, *op cit.*

The Collins family held the manor of Colwell for two generations following its purchase by William in the early seventeenth century. In 1644 it was probably placed in the hands of William's grandson and namesake William Collins, who was baptised in his mother's parish of Huntsham, Devon, on 22 November 1620. This younger William Collins married Ann Hollwaye in the middle of the Civil Wars, on 17 July 1644, at Uffculme, and the manor was part of his marriage settlement. Their marriage was also recorded in the parish registers of Offwell:

17 Jul 1644   William Collyns gent of this p[ar]ish was marryed to Ann Hollwaye of Uffculm the seventeth day of July marryed at Uffculm

The prestigious north aisle, Offwell Church

Civil War and the Commonwealth

Quiet and secluded as it is, Offwell suffered its fair share of disturbances during the Civil Wars, and the rector of the day, Thomas Jones, who had acquired the living in 1632, was an unusually outspoken and energetic Royalist, a position which brought him into direct confrontation with the puritan authorities in the 1640s; he was attacked, robbed and imprisoned and repeated plundering onslaughts were made upon the rectory. Jones, who had taken his sympathies to the extreme of fighting with Hopton's army at Devizes, where he was alleged to have killed a soldier, was finally forced to flee the country and he died in penury in Holland; he did not live to see the Restoration.[42]

William Collins predeceased his father and died while only in his thirties, in 1657, as recorded on a memorial over the family vault in Offwell church:

HERE LIETH THE BODIE OF WILLIAM COLLYNS
GENT DIED THE 31 DAY OF OCTOBER ANNO DNI 1657

---

[42] For a full account of these, see *A History of Offwell Church and Parish* (Debrett Ancestry Research, 2009), Chapter Three.

Four days before his death, on 26 October 1657, William made his will, which was proved in London in February 1658 (see Appendix C, page 113). He left 50 shillings for the poor, and 40 shillings each to his servants Zachary and Philip Chapple; smaller sums were given to some other servants. His father's 'annuity and diet agreed on between him and myself' was to be upheld; but as a young father William's principal concern was for his wife, whom he made sole executrix, and his daughters 'who are young and of tender age'. Under the terms of his marriage settlement, William was unable to appoint trustees for their education and care, but he was 'very desirous and willing that they and theire Estate should be soe disposed of and ordered as that my said daughters should be virtuously and piouslie educated and their Estate preserved and kept from wasting until they shall be of fit age and Capacitie to manage it themselves' and he requested Thomas Marwood, gentleman of Honiton, Robert Starr, gentleman of Seaton, Devon, and Andrew Ford of Offwell, to act informally to guide his widow in this respect, and to act as guardians in the event of his wife's early death.

William Collins' will also described an interesting arrangement he had made with the rector of Offwell, Revd Humphrey Bradford, for the payment of tithes that he owed the rector for his property at West Colwell:

> I give to Humphry Bradford, clerk, Rector of the parish of Offwell 50s yearly, to be paid quarterly at the birth of our Lord God, the annunciation of the blessed Virgin Mary, the nativity of St John Baptist and St Michael the Archangel, which by agreement between him and myself is to be paid and received during the life of the said Humphry Bradford while he continues Rector of the said Church, in lieu and full satisfaction of all tithes and duties whatsoever which during the said time issue or are due from one messuage or tenement with appurtenances commonly called West Colwell, otherwise Clappers Tenement, or any part thereof, in Offwell.

The will was proved on 26 February 1658 in the Prerogative Court of Canterbury.[43]

The payment (or non-payment) of tithes was a very controversial issue during the Commonwealth period; many people objected to this ancient system of providing an income to support the clergy and arrangements such as the one made between the rector Humphrey Bradford and local landowners like William Collins were the subject of much litigation.

Zachary Chapple, who as a 'servant' of William Colllins received a legacy of 40 shillings, was in fact a surgeon and physician in Offwell, and the diocesan archives of Exeter contain an unusual petition, drawn up at some point between 1662 and 1667, signed by John Copleston and the rector of Offwell, certifying to the medical skills of Zachary Chapple and requesting a continuation of his licence.[44]

In 1658 a detailed seating plan in Offwell church was drawn up; the leading inhabitants of the parish were allotted seats according to their status, and in many cases the seat belonged to a particular

---

[43] Prior to 1858, probate matters were under the jurisdiction of the church. The PCC had superior jurisdiction over all local church courts; from medieval times until 1858 it was used for wealthy testators, those who had property in more than one diocese or who had property or who died abroad. During the Commonwealth, the church courts were suspended and all probate matters had to pass through the PCC. The majority of Devon wills proved locally were destroyed during the Second World War.

[44] Devon Archives PR517/160.

property or tenement. Thus the plan is effectively a diagram of the social hierarchy in Offwell, shortly before the Restoration. Pride of place went to the Collins family, who had sole use of the east end of the north aisle, under which lay their family vault. Whoever drew up the seating plan had not taken into account the recent death of William Collins of West Colwell, who features prominently, but there was by now also a John Collins, who was the only parishioner defined on the plan as a gentleman. John Collins probably occupied Colwell House, which was possibly the ancient manor house,[45] and the plan states that 'the Ile [aisle] in the north side of the Chanchell doth absolute belong unto Colwell House and the first seat in the same side of the church'. In addition to this, the plan notes that 'the fifty seate in the midel ranke on the South side of the pillow [pillar] is unto Willi Collyns for West Colwell'. The Collins family also had 'the first pew in the middell Ranke' and four other pews, some of which would have been used for the servants in their employ.

The identity of John Collins of Colwell House is unclear but he might have been William's brother. The parish registers show that he had a wife named Mary: they had two children, John and Thomasin, but both died as infants within two weeks of each other in 1657.

During Charles II's reign an unpopular tax based on the number of hearths in each house was levied. Each house worth over twenty shillings was liable to pay a tax of two shillings per annum for each hearth or stove. The surviving returns for the year 1672 show that William's widow, Ann Collins, was living at West Colwell in a substantial house with five hearths, and John Collins of Colwell also lived in a house with five hearths.

The Heirs of William Collins

William Collins left no son but only daughters, who were 'young and of tender age' when he made his will in October 1657. Under English law, where there was no male heir, a landowner's estates were divided equally between his surviving daughters, and therefore once again we enter a period of fragmentation of the manor of Colwell. There were probably six daughters in all. The youngest two, Margaret and Elizabeth, died young: Margaret was buried on 29 October 1656, aged about seven months; and Elizabeth died in March 1658, aged about nine months.

William Collins's property was thus divided between his four surviving daughters, these being Joan who was baptised on 14 May 1645 and who married Thomas Southcott, gentleman, on 2 June 1669 at Offwell; Mary who was baptised on 4 April 1649 and married John Beare on 14 May 1674 at Buckland-Tout-Saints; Ann who was baptised on 17 April 1651 and who married in about September or October 1675 (but not at Offwell) to Richard Holway, gentleman of Priory in the parish of Broadhembury; and Dorothy who was baptised on 4 October 1653 and who married Henry Southcott on 3 July 1694 at Offwell.[46] Two of these surnames had already been linked with that of Collins in previous generations: Ann, wife of William Collins, was a Holway, and William's mother was a Be(a)re; his aunt Prudence and his uncle William also married spouses named Beare.

---

[45] See above, page 11.

[46] All these dates of baptisms, marriages and burials are taken from the parish registers of Offwell.

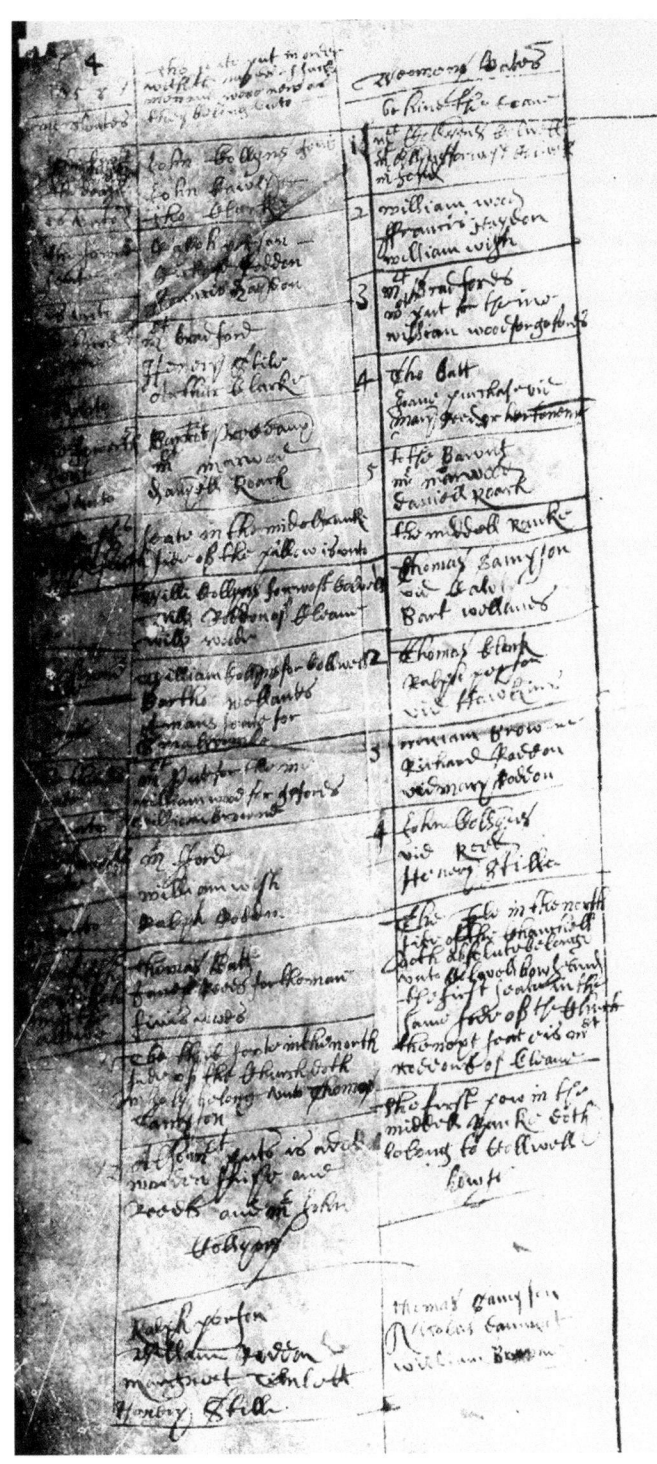

Seating Plan for Offwell Church, 1658[47]

[47] Offwell Parish Registers, Devon Archives 364A/PR/1. Reproduced with the kind permission of Devon Archives and Local Studies Service.

Joan (Collins) Southcott died in 1696, and her fine baroque memorial plaque (on the north wall of the aisle) bears witness to the wealth and status of the Southcotts:

> *HIC PROPE REQUIESCIT JOANA*
> *UXOR THOMAE SOUTHCOTT DE*
> *KILMINGTON GEN : FILIA NATU*
> *MAXIMA GUILELMI ET ANNAE*
> *COLLYNS DE COLLWELL ARMIG :*
> *OBIIT 14 DIE DECEMBRIS ANNO*
> *DOMINI 1696*

[Near here lies Joan the wife of Thomas Southcott of Kilmington, gentleman: daughter of William and Ann Collins of Colwell, armiger. Died 14 December 1696]

A second tablet, recording the burial of Joan's younger sister Dorothy, who also married a Southcott, had disappeared by the time Colonel Ramsden compiled his parish history in 1949, but was still there in about 1820. This apparently read:

> *HIC JUXTA SITA EST DOROTHEA*
> *UXOR HENRICI SOUTHCOT GEN:*
> *FILIA GULIELMI ET ANNAE COLLYNS DE*
> *COLWELL ARMIGER. HOC ETIAM SEPULCHRO*
> *UNA CUM SORORIBUS*
> *SUIS ET AVIS PRO AVIS SEPULTA*
> *OBBIT DIE 16 SEPT ANNO DNI 1698*[48]

[Near here lies Dorothy, wife of Henry Southcott, gentleman, daughter of William and Ann Collins of Colwell, armiger. Also in this vault are one of her sisters and her forefathers. Died 16 September 1698]

Dorothy was over 40 when she married, and she died four years later. The two sisters were buried in the Collins family vault, as the parish register confirms.

The division of the Collins family estates between the four heiresses is clarified by two documents held in the Marwood Elton collection at the Devon Archives. The first of these was a deed dated 24 July 1675, relating to the quarter share of Dorothy Collins.[49] The second, drawn up two months later on 29 September 1675, was the marriage settlement of Anne Collins, who was about to marry Richard Holway.[50] Both Dorothy and Mary were described as 'one of the four daughters and coheiresses of William Collins gent deceased'. Abstracts of these documents are shown at Appendix B (pages 106 to 107).

---

[48] *Devon Association Transactions*, vol 48 page 295; cited by Ramsden, *op cit*, Appendix, page 49/2.
[49] Devon Archives 210M/T/63.
[50] Devon Archives 210M/T/64.

It would appear that John and George Beare of Bearescombe, which lies in the south Devon parish of Buckland-Tout-Saints, acted as trustees for the two sisters, Anne and Dorothy Collins. The two documents show that each of William Collins's properties was divided into four parts, and each daughter was allotted one part each, thus fragmenting the inheritance into four quarters. Colwell was mentioned three times; the main part of the manor was defined as 'the Capital Messuage, Manor/Mansion House, Barton Farm, and the demesne lands of Colwell alias East Colwell'; this would imply that the manor house and what is now known as Colwell Barton formed a distinct unit. Secondly, West Colwell, which had recently been occupied by William Clapp (who was now deceased) in 1675, formed another distinct unit. Thirdly, 'the Manor or Lordship of Colwell' was divided into four; this may just have been intended to convey the title of 'lord of the manor' rather than referring to any specific property. Finally, it is worth noting that the Collins daughters were each given a quarter of 'that quarry or freestone and limestone in the parish of Widworthy heretofore purchased of Oliver Francklyn gent and Peter Francklyn gent ...'; this must surely refer to the quarry in Sutton Lucy and Widworthy which their great-grandfather purchased from the Franklin family in about 1614. There is no mention of Colwell Wood or of the Mayne family (see Chapter Three) in these documents, and thus we have no direct evidence of the Wood's status at this period, or to whom it belonged, but it is likely that it was part of the Colwell Barton estate.

William Collins died three years before the Restoration of King Charles II, an event that was still being celebrated in Offwell many years later by the ringing of bells and a service of thanksgiving; the day was referred to in the churchwardens' accounts of 1694 as the day 'whinn the King com hom'.[51]

Thus we can see that during the first half of the seventeenth century the Collins family gradually reconstructed the fragmented manor of Colwell to establish a comfortable country estate, with income not only from its land but also from the stone quarry nearby at Widworthy; only to see it broken up again, into four pieces, on the untimely death of William Collins in 1657.

---

[51] See our *History of Offwell Church and Parish* (2009), page 52.

Chapter Three

THE EIGHTEENTH CENTURY

As we have seen, in 1658 the ownership of Colwell was divided between the four young daughters of William Collins, who all subsequently married: Joan Southcott, Dorothy Southcott, Ann Holway and Mary Beare. The estate thus passed into the eighteenth century in a fragmented state, and the documentation for this period is sparse, with many pieces of evidence missing. The surnames Beare and Holway disappear from the records relating to Colwell, which suggests that two of the Collins heiresses, Ann Holway and Mary Beare (Mary had two sons and a daughter in 1706), either died without surviving male issue or sold their portions. Instead, we find portions of Colwell being owned by the families of Southcott, Mayne and Marwood throughout the eighteenth century. All three families were wealthy local gentry in Devon, and their lands in Offwell formed only a small part of their overall estates.

The Southcott Family

The Southcott family were residents in Offwell and took an active interest in parish affairs. At a special meeting of parishioners held at Offwell on 25 May 1697, we find the names 'Tho Southcott' and 'Henry Southcott' listed among those attending; these were the two men who had married the Collins heiresses Joan and Dorothy. As we have seen in Chapter Two, both their wives died in the 1690s and handsome memorials were raised to them in Offwell church.

In 1700 both Henry and Thomas Southcott appeared (with James Sheppard) as defendants in a Chancery case concerning the land and personal estate of 'the deceased Anne Collings' in Offwell. The plaintiffs were Michael Hayman and his wife Anne.[52] Michael and Ann Hayman were relatives of the Collins family and they sold a house next to Offwell church to the rector, Robert Rous, in 1726.[53] Three years later, in 1703, the same estate of Anne Collings, deceased (but now the description included the tolls and fairs in Axminster, Devon) was again the subject of a Chancery suit; the defendants were again Henry and Thomas Southcott (this time with Richard Hallett) but the plaintiffs were now the Beare family: John Beare, Mary Beare his wife, Elizabeth Beare infant, Frances Beare infant and Thomas Beare infant. This family group must have been Mary, née Collins, her husband and children. It would thus appear that the disposal of Anne's share of the Colwell estate was a contentious matter and possibly the Southcotts had taken possession of it.

Henry Southcott, Dorothy's widower, was certainly living in Offwell, probably at West Colwell, when he died in 1706. He left a will (see Appendix C, page 116) dated 1 April 1706 and proved in the Prerogative Court of Canterbury on 8 November of the same year. He asked to be buried in the

---

[52] The National Archives C 6/349/53. The papers have not been examined.
[53] See our *History of Offwell Church and Parish* (2009), page 60.

family vault at Offwell, which was to be enlarged 'that I may lye by the side of my deceased wife'. The will deals only with his personal estate, so his portion of the Colwell estate, if he still had it, was evidently taken care of elsewhere. The minor bequests in the will provide a glimpse into Henry's prosperous, though not opulent, household in Offwell in the reign of Queen Anne, with his silver porringer, cups and plate (one plate had his wife Mary's coat of arms in the middle). This was however still the will of a gentleman farmer, and as an afterthought he bequeathed to Luke Pitman and Mary Long, who had already received bequests of £5, 'a cow to each'.

It was customary to remember the poor of the parish in a gentleman's will, but Henry Southcott was more specific in this regard than most: he left £20 for the benefit of those poor of Offwell 'who by reason of their poverty and hard labour doe keep themselves from the relief of the said Parish'. The interest of this sum was to be distributed annually on Christmas Day by 'four of the best people of the parish of Offwell'. Here was a reminder of the significance of the parish hierarchy, and perhaps we may detect a hint of resentment at the levying of parish rates. These fluctuated greatly and recent figures had been high (more than £72 for the parish for the year 1704).

Other bequests included legacies of £10 each to Elizabeth, Francis and Thomas Beare, children of Henry's sister-in-law Mary Beare, née Collins. Dorothy Collins had married relatively late in life and lived for only four years after marrying. She and Henry had no children, but there was certainly a second generation of Southcotts in Offwell, so these were perhaps the children of Thomas and Joan Southcott.

This second generation of Southcotts has not been investigated, but we have a few clues to their identities. In a rate levied by the parish of Offwell in April 1708 to provide for poor relief, 'the occupiers of Colwell' were asked to contribute 2s 7d, but unfortunately they were not named. In a list of donors to a parish apprenticeship scheme of 1722, George Southcott was the third name to be mentioned. In 1725 Dorothy Southcott and Henry Southcott each contributed the large sum of £20 towards the purchase of a field in Offwell, the income from which was to be applied for the relief of poor labourers. A century later, Samuel and Daniel Lysons in their county history *Magna Britannica*, which was published in 1822,[54] noted that:

> West Colwell, which had been several years in the Southcote family, has recently been purchased by the Rev. Dr. Copleston, Provost of Oriel College, in Oxford.

There were still Southcotts in Offwell at the time of the 1901 census.

The Mayne Family (1680–1726)

In the meantime, by 1680, a portion of Colwell (including Colwell Wood) had somehow passed into the hands of John Mayne, a merchant of Exeter, who drew up a lengthy will on 30 May 1680, being evidently at the end of his life, for it was proved less than a month later. A summary of this will is shown at Appendix C (pages 114 to 115).

---

[54] This was based on questionnaires circulated to individual parishes.

John Mayne was a very prosperous and public-spirited merchant in Exeter, the son of Richard Mayne, a linen draper, and his wife Elizabeth; he was baptised at St Petrock's on 22 January 1624 along with his brother Thomas, probably a twin. They had two younger brothers (Samuel and Zachary) and three sisters (Elizabeth, Prudence who died in infancy, and another Prudence who survived).

Richard Mayne had drawn up a brief and probably hasty will on 7 September 1627, being then 'sicke of bodie', and at the time his wife was expecting another child (Samuel, baptised on 25 November 1627). However, the will was not proved until 22 January 1646. It makes no mention of any property other than personal estate and thus sheds no light on how the Mayne family acquired their interest in Colwell.

John's brother Zachary (baptised 1631) was educated at Christ Church, Oxford, and on graduating became an Independent preacher and schoolmaster, but in later life he conformed to the Church of England, although he was never ordained in the Anglican church.[55]

John's younger brother Samuel Mayne of Exeter (baptised in 1627) left a will which was proved in the Prerogative Court of Canterbury in February 1662.[56]

John Mayne asked to be buried alongside his parents in the church of St Petrock, Exeter. His lands went to his only surviving son[57] Christopher Mayne for his lifetime, and thereafter to his male heirs. Christopher also received the enormous sum of £8,000. Neither Colwell nor Offwell was mentioned specifically; our evidence that John Mayne owned Colwell Wood at this date comes from a conveyance drawn up over a century later, in 1798,[58] and it is possible that this was inaccurate.

John Mayne also left an only daughter, Elizabeth, and at the time of his final illness, negotiations were in progress with Sir Charles Wolseley concerning the marriage of Elizabeth to Sir Charles's son and heir.[59] Elizabeth was left her own fortune of £6,000. John also left Elizabeth the bed 'now in my Purple Chamber where my late wife dyed', as well as her late mother's jewels and bracelets, half the plate, and the coach and horses. This gives evidence of a city lifestyle somewhat different to the simpler life of the Southcotts in Offwell.

John Mayne was clearly close to his brother Zachary, and he gave a generous allowance of £50 a year to Zachary's son, Gabriel Mayne, 'from the time he shall be settled in any university there to reside and to study the Art, Faculty or Science of Physicke', for as many as seven years, if that was how

---

[55] Bertha Porter, 'Mayne, Zachary (1631–1694)', revised by H J McLachlan, *Oxford Dictionary of National Biography* (Oxford University Press, 2004). A lengthy account of the career of Zachary Mayne was also published in *Transactions of the Devon Association*, vol 126 (1994), pages 181–197: 'Zachary Mayne 1631–1694' by Ann Sheridan. This makes no mention of Colwell. Zachary's will was proved on 24 July 1695 in the PCC.

[56] The National Archives PROB 11/307/275. This brief will mentions the testator's brothers John and Zachary and his brother-in-law George Wills, who had married Prudence Mayne.

[57] The parish registers of St Petrock show that John had other children who died in infancy named Faith, John and Prudence.

[58] Kinglake and Newman family papers, Somerset Heritage Centre (South West Heritage Trust) DD\AY/348.

[59] If this was Sir Charles Wolseley of Wolseley, 2nd baronet, his heir in 1680 was his eldest son Robert (born 1650), but Robert died unmarried in 1697.

THE MAYNE FAMILY

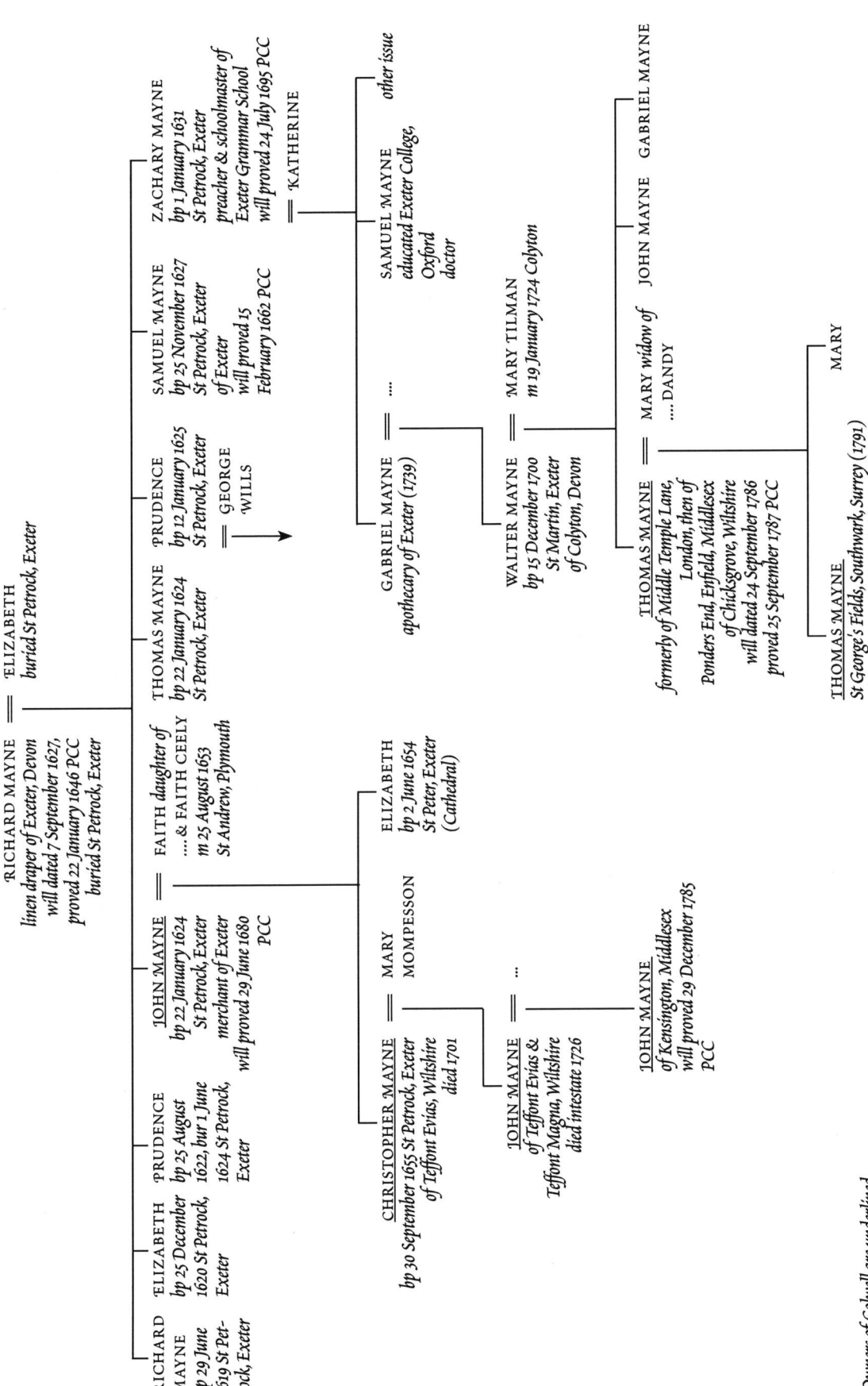

Owners of Colwell are underlined

long it took Gabriel to complete his medical studies. Gabriel was however to provide for his brothers and sisters out of this annuity, should both their parents die. We know from a reference to Gabriel Mayne in a Chancery proceeding dated 1739 that he did indeed become an apothecary in Exeter,[60] but he was not apparently a graduate of Oxford or Cambridge University. Another of Zachary's sons, Samuel, went to Exeter College, Oxford, and became a doctor.

John Mayne had a particular interest in education, and he also left £400 to buy land in Exeter for a school (which was to be administered by the Mayor) and schoolmaster's house; a further endowment of £1,000 was to provide the salaries of the resident schoolmaster and visiting writing master, and books for the scholars. The school was to be for 'Forty boyes whose Parents shall be esteemed not well able to pay for their schooling' and 'twenty Boyes more whose Parents may be able to pay for their schooling, and noe more'; John's name and coat of arms were to be engraved in brass or stone and displayed outside the school, and his brother Zachary[61] was to be one of several named governors. The aim was to ready the boys for apprenticeships. This was all to be done within two years; the project had evidently already been set in motion, for Mayne was already paying a schoolmaster (Francis Fryer) and provision was made for this to continue until the new school was built.

Not content with this foundation, John Mayne was also generous in endowing schools in several maritime towns in Devon (Topsham, Dartford, Barnstaple and Bideford), where he was keen to encourage the study of navigation as well as reading, writing and 'ciphering' (arithmetic).

It thus appears that John Mayne's only surviving son, Christopher Mayne, inherited (for life) a portion of Colwell in 1680, together with a legacy of £8,000. Despite this large sum, by February 1694 we find him using his Colwell property as security for a mortgage, the sum borrowed being £2,100 (from James Crosse, a merchant in Southampton). The deed itself has not been found, but it is referred to in a later mortgage deed drawn up in 1714.[62] It would appear from the terms of the 1694 mortgage that Christopher Mayne owned three-quarters of the 'Manors or Lordshipps of Colwell and Offwell' by this date. In addition, he owned three-quarters of 'the Capital Messuage Barton Farm and demesne called East Colwell'. This is confirmed by another mortgage dated 7 February 1693, again with James Crosse of Southampton, which refers to 'three quarters of the manors and lordships of Colwell and Offwell in Offwell and Widworthy' as well as the quarry in Widworthy and other lands in Offwell, and the 'liberty to dig marl in Longhurst etc'.[63] The manorial property was defined by a deed of about 1614, when it was sold by the Franklin family to William Collins; this would suggest that there was no intervening sale of Colwell, which in turn might imply that Christopher's father John Mayne acquired his three-quarter share of Colwell through inheritance or marriage, rather than by purchase; but how this came about, we do not know. His wife was Faith Ceely, who came from a merchant family of Plymouth and elsewhere in Devon.

---

[60] The National Archives C 11/657/7.

[61] Zachary Mayne was Master of Exeter Grammar School in 1690, but this was not his brother's foundation.

[62] Devon Archives 210M/T95A.

[63] Royal Institution of Cornwall HT/1/48: Catalogue entry in The Discovery Catalogue, TNA.

Some of Mayne's debts probably relate to legal expenses, for he was a litigant in several Chancery cases in the 1690s, relating to property in Wiltshire, Devon and to other matters elsewhere.[64]

Christopher Mayne was described in the deeds as a resident of Teffont Evias, which lies about three miles east of the town of Tisbury, Wiltshire. He died in 1701 and we have no evidence that he ever lived at Colwell. He was succeeded by his son, John Mayne of Teffont Evias, who paid off £1,000 of the 1694 mortgage, but in December 1711 transferred the mortgage, with an additional loan, presumably secured on the same property, to John Jelfe, a merchant in Bristol.

In October 1720 John Mayne broke the entail that had been created in his grandfather's will 40 years earlier. He died intestate in 1726, leaving just one son, John Mayne esquire junior, who was described as of Kensington, Middlesex.

A lease (part of a lease and release conveyance)[65] survives from 1725 whereby John Mayne of Teffont Magna (which adjoins Teffont Evias) leased a cottage in Colwell, which had previously been occupied by Ralph Chapple, to William Gill, gentleman of Honiton, for one year:[66]

> **Lease for one year**
> 29 November 1725
> 1) John Mayne of Teffont Magna, Wiltshire, Esq, son and heir of
> Christopher Mayne Esq deceased
> 2) William Gill of Honiton, gent
> Consideration: 5s
> Property: All that cottage house and garden lying at Colwell in the parish of Offwell now in the possession of Ralph Chapple with appurtenances, during the term of one year
> Signature of John Mayne

As we shall see, it was in this year that the Marwood family acquired most of the Mayne family property in Colwell.

The Marwood Family

The Marwood family was a distinguished one locally: Thomas Marwood, who was said to have been born in about 1512 and died in September 1617 at the remarkable age of 105, was a physician to Queen Elizabeth.[67] We have already seen that William Collins (who died in 1657) requested in his will[68] that 'my very good friend Thomas Marwood, gentleman of Honiton' should assist his widow in the bringing up of his daughters.

---

[64] The Discovery Catalogue, TNA: the proceedings have not been examined.

[65] Lease and release was a common form of conveyance in the eighteenth century. The vendor leased the property to the purchaser for a nominal sum (usually five shillings and at peppercorn rent), the intention being to give the purchaser actual possession of the property to be conveyed. On the following day the vendor released all his interests in the property, and this is usually the more informative of the two documents.

[66] Devon Archives 281M/T76.

67 *Burke's Landed Gentry* (1952): see our pedigree chart of the Marwood-Elton family, below, page 79.

[68] See Appendix C, page 104.

The Marwood family was already taking an active part in parish life in Offwell by the 1720s. In 1722 action was taken to provide apprenticeships for poor children of the parish; this was an effective way of lifting families out of poverty. The major landowners all took responsibility for a child (which required them to pay £40), and men of lesser means joined together with smaller sums to sponsor an apprenticeship. This provides us with a cross-section of the Offwell hierarchy, and the following men headed the list, each providing funding for one child. The names are listed in strict social order, with the baronet at the top of the list followed by two 'esquires' and then six 'gentlemen':

> Sir Edmond Prideaux
> John Maine Esq
> George Southcott Esq
> James Marwood gent

On 14 May 1744 Thomas Marwood appeared at the top of a list of parishioners who resolved a dispute with the churchwardens over 'extravagant charges' in the repair of Offwell church and the church house, but there was no one called Mayne or Southcott acting with him on this occasion.

In 1725 it appears that Thomas Marwood, who lived at Sutton in the parish of Widworthy, bought East Colwell (also known as Colwell), Colwell Mills and other small properties in Colwell from John Mayne. The lease and release by which this sale took place has not been found, but the conveyance is referred to in a marriage settlement drawn up on 27 June 1734,[69] in anticipation of the marriage between James Marwood (son of Thomas) to Sarah Sealy, the daughter of Samuel Sealy of Avishayes,[70] Chaffcombe, near Chard, Somerset. (Whether this family was related to that of Faith Ceely, wife of John Mayne, we do not know.) By the terms of the settlement, the Marwood family placed several valuable properties in trust, and embedded in the description of the properties we find the earliest specific reference to Colwell Wood itself:

> ... All that capital messuage mansion house barton and demesnes of East Colwell (or Colwell alias East Colwell)
> ... all that coppice called Scannel Coppice thereunto belonging
> ... all that dwelling house and water grist mill called Colwell Mills and those two cottages called Chapples Cottage and Hewett's Cottage with orchards thereunto belonging, all of which last mentioned were heretofore part and parcel of the Manor of Colwell in the said parish of Offwell
> ... two meadows called Deymond's Meadows als Carselake Meadows (10a) in Widworthy with liberty for digging marl[71] in one acre of a close called Long Hurst
> ... property in Stockland, Dorset
> ... land in Upottery, Devon
> ... a messuage called Bear Hill in Church Taunton parish, Devon
> ... a messuage called Chuttleton in Hemiock, Devon
> ... a messuage called Dunkeswell Abbey in the parish of Dunkeswell, Devon

---

[69] Devon Archives 281M/T387 and T388.

[70] This mansion, built in the seventeenth century but remodelled in the eighteenth, still stands.

[71] Marl is a loose deposit of clay and calcium carbonate, used as a soil improver. Christopher Mayne used his 'liberty to dig marl in Longhurst etc' as security for a mortgage in 1693 (see Chapter Three).

...   a messuage called Ashwell in Ilminster, Somerset

...   all other messuages lands etc whereof Thomas Marwood is in possession

'**Except** and always reserved out of this present grant and conveyance unto Thomas Marwood his heirs and assigns All that Quarry of Freestone or Lymestone commonly called or known by the name of Colwell Quarry scituat lying and being in Widworthy aforesaid **And also except** all that wood or Coppice commonly called or known by the name of Colwell Wood and all hedges trees and woods to the same belonging in such manner as the same was and is excepted in and by one Indenture of Release bearing date the seven and twentieth day of March 1725 made or mentioned to be made between John Mayne of Teffont Magna in the county of Wiltshire, son and heir of Christopher Mayne Esq his late deceased father of the one part and the said Thomas Marwood of the other part'

Granted in trust to Thomas Drake and John Lyddon, income to James Marwood for his life and then to his wife Sarah, now Sealy.

Signatures and seals of Thomas Marwood, James Marwood, Samuel Sealy, Sarah Sealy, Thomas Drake, John Lyddon.

By June 1734, then, the Marwood family were the owners of Colwell 'mansion house' (also known as East Colwell), together with Scannel Coppice, Colwell Mills, Chapple's Cottage and Hewett's Cottage. West Colwell had remained in the hands of the Southcott family. 'Chapple's Cottage' would seem to be the same property that John Mayne sold in November 1725 to William Gill (see above, page 37), so perhaps the Marwoods had acquired this separately from William Gill.

The last clause in the 1734 marriage settlement is most significant with regard to the history of Colwell Wood. It shows that when John Mayne sold his Colwell property to the Marwoods in 1725, he retained ownership of the quarry in Sutton Lucy and Colwell Wood. This association of Colwell with the quarry at Sutton Lucy can be clearly seen from the early seventeenth century sale of the manor by the Franklin family to William Collins; it is likely that the quarry had been a detached part of the manor of Colwell from the late medieval period. The motive behind the detachment of the wood and quarry from the main body of Colwell manor is not entirely clear, but we may speculate that the non-resident Mayne family wished to retain them as profitable business interests; since there was no house to maintain in either the wood or the quarry, they could be managed from a distance.

To summarise a complicated and obscure chapter in the history of Colwell, we can postulate that at some point between 1675 and 1694, three-quarters of the manor of Colwell (including Colwell Wood) passed into the hands of Christopher Mayne, probably by inheritance from his father John. Christopher's son, John Mayne, sold his share in 1725 to Thomas Marwood, retaining Colwell Wood and the quarry in Widworthy, but he died a year later without leaving a will.

From this point on we are concerned only with the history of Colwell Wood and Colwell Wood Cottage, and thus we return to the Mayne family.

The Mayne family (1726–1787)

As we have seen, when John Mayne of Teffont Magna died in 1726, he had already sold off most of his Colwell estate, retaining only Colwell Quarry and Colwell Wood. His heir was his son and namesake, John Mayne of Kensington. This John Mayne is unlikely to have had much interest in the community of Offwell but as a landowner he was nevertheless required to contribute financially.

The churchwardens' accounts for Offwell contain a list of properties and their owners who were assessed for land tax on 2 April 1763 at the rate of four shillings in the pound: this shows that 'John Main Esq' was still the owner of Colwell Wood, and was required to pay £1 18s 3d. In November 1767, the scheme to provide places for poor apprentices in Offwell was repeated, and the churchwardens' accounts show that 'Colwell estate' agreed to contribute £40 per annum to finance an apprentice. John Main esquire 'for Colwell Wood' was to contribute £14 per annum towards this sum.

In June 1773, a list of church rates levied in Offwell shows three separate Colwell entries; this clearly shows what were now three separate properties, in their hierarchical order:

Benedictus Marwood Esq for Colwell Estate	13s 6d (with other smaller properties)
Michael Southcott Esq for West Colwell	3s 3s (with other smaller properties)
John Main Esq for Colwell Wood	1s 9d[72]

John Mayne junior was apparently the last descendant of his great-grandfather and namesake John Mayne of Exeter (died 1680). We do not know exactly when he died, but he left a will proved in the Prerogative Court of Canterbury on 29 December 1785. A lease and release dated 16 March 1798,[73] which is the source of much of our information about the Mayne family and their interest in Colwell Wood, makes it clear that on his death his estate was inherited by his third cousin, Thomas Mayne esquire of Enfield, north Middlesex. Thomas was the son of Walter Mayne of Colyton, Devon, and Walter was the son of Gabriel Mayne of Exeter. Gabriel was the son of Zachary Mayne of Exeter, the Independent minister and school teacher.

Thomas Mayne of Enfield, who thus inherited Colwell Wood from his cousin John at the very end of 1785, held it only briefly. He made his own lengthy will on 24 September 1786, but with no specific mention of Colwell or Offwell. A brief abstract of this will is shown at Appendix C.

News of Thomas Mayne's death seems to have come late to Offwell, for the churchwardens' accounts for the year 1791 (four years after his death) remark:

Mr Main in arrears for Colwell Woods   1s 9d

Thomas's main property outside London and Middlesex was referred to in his will as 'Cheeks Grove'; this can be identified as Chicksgrove, which lies less than a mile from Teffont Evias and Sutton Mandeville, near Tisbury, Wiltshire. Thomas appointed his friends Samuel Stennett and Charles Lucas to be trustees to raise a total of £6,000 from his freehold estates in order to provide

---

[72] Churchwardens' accounts, Offwell: Devon Archives 364A/PW3.
[73] Kinglake and Newman Family Papers, Somerset Heritage Centre DD\AY/348: see Appendix B.

for his children; it was these directions to trustees that caused his Colwell estate to be sold by auction after his death. Thomas gave his wife Mary an annuity of £100, and instructed the trustees to raise £3,000 for his daughter, also called Mary. He left a son, Thomas Mayne junior, who was described in a deed of 1798 as of the parish of Sutton Mandeville, about ten miles west of Salisbury, Wiltshire. Thomas Mayne junior and his father's trustees thus became the joint owners of Colwell Wood.

However, it appears that there were problems in settling the estate of Thomas Mayne senior; he may have left insufficient funds to cover the legacies he left in his will, and this also might explain why the church rates went unpaid. The case went to the court of Chancery, which dealt with a huge volume of litigation relating to disputed wills, trusts and property transactions. The Chancery action was brought by Thomas Mayne junior against his father's trustees, Charles Lucas and Samuel Stennett; it seems likely that Thomas was resisting the sale of Colwell and other property which he believed was his by inheritance. On 18 February 1793 the Chancery court ordered that part of the testator's estate should be sold by auction to the highest bidder; among these properties was Colwell Wood, which was purchased by Thomas Graves (later Admiral Sir Thomas Graves) for the sum of £1,210. The Offwell church rate list of 30 May 1795 records the following item:

Thomas Graves Esqr for Colwell Wood   1s 9d[74]

Church rates were assessed on all lands within the parish; the sums raised were used to repair the church and its property. This listing indicates that Thomas Graves had already taken possession of the Wood by 1795. The Chancery documents, which consist of ten very large parchment sheets, have been briefly examined; these constituted the pleadings in the case.[75] These have not been analysed in any detail, but the sequence was as follows:

Mayne (plaintiff) *v* **Stennett (defendant)**
1) **Petition** dated 24 January 1791 of Thomas Mayne of St George's Fields, Surrey, gentleman, only son and heir at law named in will of Thomas Mayne formerly of   Middle Temple Lane, London
2) **Amended Petition** (dated as above)
3) **Answer** of Samuel Stennett, a Defendant, dated 26 June 1792
4) **Further Petition** of Thomas Mayne, dated 16 May 1792
5) **Answer** of John Thomas Mayne, infant, dated 2 July 1792
6) **Answer** of John Allen and wife Mary, Defendants, dated 16 August 1792
7) **Joint and Several Answers** of William Ellis Wrench and wife Mary, dated 26 April 1792
8) **Answer** of Charles Lucas, Defendant, dated 26 April 1792

Readers of Charles Dickens' novel, *Bleak House,* will recognise how protracted Chancery actions were at this period, with very verbose pleadings, lengthy procedures, interim orders, reports and directions before a final judgement was eventually given. This case appears to have been no exception, and the above listing refers only to the pleadings, and does not include court orders or

---

[74] Churchwardens' accounts, Offwell: Devon Archives 364A/PW3.
[75] Court of Chancery Proceedings, 1758 to 1800: The National Archives C 12 184/10.

judgements, which were filed separately. We do not know exactly when the auction to sell Colwell took place, but it was probably shortly after the Chancery order of 18 February 1793 and certainly before 30 April 1794. Thomas Graves would thus have paid the large sum of £1,210 at least four years before 'completion' took place by the deeds of 16/17 March 1798 when his title was formally granted. This sequence of events agrees with the land tax returns for Colwell Wood, which show John Mayne as the proprietor in the period 1780 to 1786, and Thomas Mayne (senior and then junior) between 1787 and 1797.

A plan was drawn up, probably to accompany the conveyance of 1798, entitled 'A Plan of Colwell Wood, the Property of Thos Graves Esqr.'[76] (see below, page 43). As a note on the plan explains, 'The Wood is Divided into 21 Parts and each part contains 2a 0r 27p, which makes in the whole 45a 2r 7p'. At the southern edge of the wood is a path, which represents the entrance to the wood.

Somebody has marked three areas in pencil, possibly representing ponds. That somebody has also marked out an asymmetrical plot to the west of the centre line (along which there was probably already some sort of track). That plot can be identified as the site of Colwell Wood Cottage.

We have found no evidence as to who managed the woods as a tenant in Colwell until the name William Seaman appears on the land tax lists as the occupier of Colwell Wood between 1782 and 1787. William Seaman's job as manager of the woods is apparent from an announcement in the *Exeter Flying Post* of 2 May 1786:

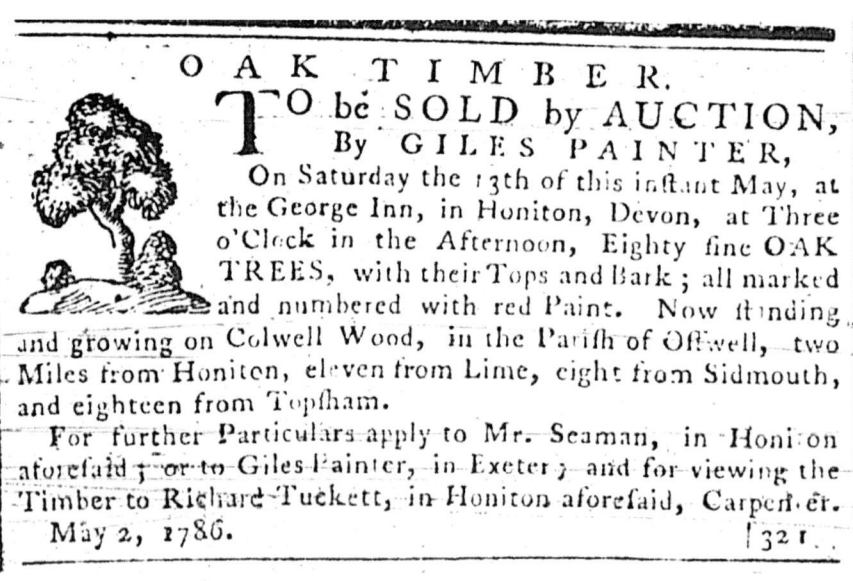

Advertisement for timber from the Exeter Flying Post, 2 May 1786

---

[76] Somerset Heritage Centre DD\AY/348.

Plan of Colwell Wood ca 1798[77]

[77] Kinglake and Newman Family Papers, Somerset Heritage Centre, DD\AY/348.

CHAPTER THREE: THE EIGHTEENTH CENTURY

At this time much oak timber was being felled for ship-building and fetched good prices. In the second half of the eighteenth century the Royal Navy was greatly expanded; after the American War of Independence, which ended in 1783, stocks of timber particularly needed replenishing, and no doubt Thomas Mayne was eager to take advantage of the opportunity. Although the land tax returns show Thomas as the 'occupier' as well as the 'proprietor' of Colwell Wood between 1789 and 1797, it is most unlikely that he lived there. William Seaman and Richard Tuckett, the carpenter, who had probably selected the trees, were both of Honiton. Colwell Wood Cottage was not yet in existence, but was to be built in the first decade of the next century.

Chapter Four

THE NINETEENTH CENTURY

Woodland and ship-building in Devon

A common theme of those who wrote about Colwell and Offwell in the eighteenth and nineteenth centuries was their woodlands, which were at this date an important economic asset. For instance, Richard Polwhele, in his *History of Devonshire* (published in three volumes between 1793 and 1806) stated that:

> The most flourishing trees are oak and ash. And here is a coppice-wood of about 100 acres … The farms are, in general, small, with orchards to each, in tolerable cultivation. The inhabitants of the parish amount to about 300 – paupers in constant pay about 20 – numbers of labourers 24, of freeholders 6. The other occupiers of estates are at rack rent. The inhabitants are, for the most part, healthy, robust, and long-lived. They hold their revel in September.

Polwhele's observations about Offwell and Colwell were probably made in the 1780s, just at the time of the auction of Colwell's timber (see Chapter Three). Coppicing, as noted here, was the traditional method of woodland management in Devon, probably since Roman times, and in the eighteenth and early nineteenth centuries much of Devon's woodland was being heavily coppiced; the practice began to die out in the middle of the nineteenth century.[78]

The newspaper announcement of the auction of timber in May 1786 provides interesting clues as to the use to which Colwell's 'eighty fine oak trees' would be put: the advertisement states that Colwell was eleven miles from Lyme Regis, eight from Sidmouth and eighteen from Topsham. All three places were ports with a ship and boat-building industry, although in the cases of Sidmouth and Lyme Regis this was on a relatively small scale. The port of Topsham, which lies on the east bank of the River Exe about four miles south of Exeter, was a much more important centre, and the ship-building industry expanded very rapidly there in the period 1800 to 1840. During the seventeenth and eighteenth centuries, Topsham was a significant port, mainly for exporting wool, which was brought from the inland parishes of south and east Devon. This had been recognised, as we have seen, by John Mayne, who in his will of 1680 included Topsham among those towns which received a bequest to help set up a school that would teach, among other things, the art of navigation. Criminals bound for Virginia and Botany Bay (Australia) also embarked at Topsham.

An important source for Topsham's industrial history is the 'Memoranda Book of Daniel Bishop Davy'; the Davy family dominated ship-building and commerce in Topsham during the first half of

---

[78] Daniel J Franklin, 'The Productive Potential of Ancient Oak-Coppice Woodland in Britain', *Rural Development Forestry Network Paper 15d* (Summer 1993).

the nineteenth century.[79] Daniel Bishop Davy's father, Robert Davy (born 1762), founded the business, but he was more than just a shipbuilder; he traded large quantities of oak timber and bark; he was a farmer and grazier; he was also a coal merchant, and he developed a large lime-burning industry. The Davy family certainly had a small ship-building yard in Sidmouth as well as Topsham. Before 1800, they mainly served the local maritime trade, building crafts such as fishing smacks and coastal cargo boats, but from 1803 onwards they secured valuable commissions to build warships for the Royal Navy. Up to this time, Plymouth was the Navy's only ship-building port in Devon, but during the Napoleonic Wars the demand for ships was great, and Topsham quickly rivalled Plymouth. Davy's shipyards built 28 naval vessels in the period 1803 to 1815. Their frames were made entirely from oak, and oak planking was used inside and outside. Elm was used to make the keel, and imported Norwegian fir was used for the deck planking, but the predominant material was oak. Once the vessels were built, they were taken to either Plymouth or Portsmouth to be fitted out for sea. The pace at which these naval ships were built was impressive: for instance, in 1814 alone, HMS *Hind* and HMS *Tyne* were completed by Davy and sailed from Exmouth. He was very proud of the quality of timber used for all his ships, and also that all his naval contracts were completed on time; he sometimes gained a bonus from the Navy for delivering ahead of the time agreed. Davy was by no means the only ship-builder on the Exe estuary in the early years of the nineteenth century, although he was certainly the most successful. His rivals included Obadiah Ayles, Thomas Owen and Tilney Rising, all of whom were based in Topsham, while John Bass was based just to the south at Lymstone.

Clearly, a very important aspect of the ship-building business was securing good sources of oak within reasonable reach of Topsham. Daniel Bishop Davy's notebook reveals how he travelled in Devon, Dorset and Hampshire, seeking out good quality oak; he commented, usually very critically, on the size and quality of timber used by his rivals, and said that only Mr Good of Bridport's timber was 'nearly equal to ours'. Ship-building timber was bought and sold by the load, and as the following contemporary definition shows, this was not a precise term:

> All timber is bought and sold by the load, and a load is 50 feet, which is supposed to weigh a ton, or 20 hundred weight; but some reckon 40 feet of rough or unhewn timber to the load; for they say, that, as hewn is measured by the square, it is very nearly exact; but rough timber, being measured by the girt (or quarter compass), which is more than one-fifth less than exact, therefore, in buying and selling of timber, it amounts to much the same, whether it is measured to the girt, at 40 feet solid to the load, or measured exactly at 50 feet to a load, the price being in proportion. In the King's yard 40 feet of hewn timber is reckoned a ton, and 50 feet of such timber goes to a load.[80]

Various prices are recorded, ranging from £6 per load for oak, to £8 15s for large Navy timber. Transporting such large pieces of timber through the countryside to the shipyards was a hazardous

[79] For this section we are indebted to Clive N Ponsford, ed, *Ship-building on the Exe: The Memoranda Book of Daniel Bishop Davy (1799–1874)*, Devon and Cornwall Record Society, new series, vol 31, 1988; and Leonard E Braddick, 'The Port of Topsham: its ships and ship-building', *Transactions of the Devon Association*, vol 85, 1953).

[80] J W Norie, *The Shipwright's Vade-Mecum* (1822), page 65.

and testing operation. The inhabitants of Topsham certainly suffered from this heavy traffic and in 1843 they passed an ordinance forbidding timbers, masts, spars and suchlike to be dragged through the town except on wheel-carriages.

The churchwardens' accounts show how closely the patriotic parishioners of Offwell followed the course of the Napoleonic Wars, particularly in respect of the Navy; prayers of thanksgiving were said on receiving news of the victories of Nelson and other British admirals. They were also instructed to tighten their belts as blockades prevented the import of food and supplies from abroad.

However, the defeat of Napoleon can hardly have been welcomed by the ship-builders of Topsham, since there were no more contracts from the Royal Navy, and Davy's business now returned to the maritime market, constructing about six or eight merchant ships a year in the period 1814 to 1819. In the 1820s and 1830s, there was a demand for schooners and East-Indiamen. One of the East-Indiamen built in Davy's shipyard, the *Batavia*, first sailed from London to Madras and Bengal in June 1810 under Captain J Mayne; perhaps he was a descendant of the Mayne family who had owned Colwell Wood. In 1819, after the naval boom was over, Daniel travelled to the east coast of England, attempting to sell timber there and taking samples of oak and elm with him, but apparently this venture was not a success.

The traffic between Offwell and Topsham was not all one way. At the end of the Wars, in 1815, the parish church accounts record that:

> In this year the Roof of the South side were all taken down the Timber Work being all very much decayed the whole of the Roof entirely new.

Several thousand slates were brought in for this from Topsham, and the company Follett & Co of Topsham also supplied three pieces of Norway fir (£15 15s). However, other timber, as might be expected, was bought from the locals: the accounts show that Nathaniel Stocker sold the church 'an oak 33ft where it lay' for £4 13s 6d, and churchwarden Emanuel Dommett, who owned several properties in the parish including 'Oadpools', contributed several oak trees whose length totalled 229 feet, for which he was paid £31 9s 9d; he also supplied oak lathes 'made out of my timber' (£3 9s). Nathaniel Stocker[81] is listed in land tax returns in 1800 and 1801 as the occupier of Colwell Wood, and thus it may be that at least one of the Colwell Wood oaks played its part in supporting the church roof at this date.

Ship-building was not, of course, the only possible use for Colwell's 'eighty fine Oak trees, with their Tops and Barks'. Oak was particularly important in house-building for beams and structural supports, and in areas where there was little brick or stone, timber was also used for cladding and weatherboarding, but this did not apply to East Devon, where stone was plentiful. It was also a vital raw material for all the mining industries, for the construction of pit props. A great deal of oak was also used to make domestic furniture, and for making a wide range of simple household and

---

[81] 'Nathaniel Stocker the younger', possibly the son of this Nathaniel, was evicted from Offwell by a removal order in 1824. Such orders were made to protect the parish from possible claims on the poor rates, and Nathaniel would have been sent back to his parish of settlement.

husbandry items, such as platters in the kitchen, farm tools and fencing. Large areas of oak wood in England were coppiced for fuel for the iron industry where coal was not available, and huge quantities of oak bark were used in the tanning industry. These industries were not prevalent in Devon, but there was virtually no coal there, and so wood also served as an extremely important and valuable source for industrial and domestic fuel; the 'tops' of the felled oaks would probably have been sold as firewood. The inhabitants of Offwell were fortunate in having a good supply of woodland close at hand for winter fuel, although its collection for this purpose might have been jealously guarded by the landowner. Similarly, the local farmers and husbandmen in Offwell and Colwell would probably have been allowed to let their pigs loose in the woodland during the autumn, although we have found no direct evidence of any such rights of pannage.

Sir Thomas Graves

Thomas Graves, who, as we have seen in the previous chapter, purchased Colwell Wood formally in 1798, provides a further link between Colwell Wood and the Royal Navy, in which he had a long and distinguished career, rising to be a full admiral; this has earned him a place in the *Oxford Dictionary of National Biography*.[82] A younger son of a Londonderry family, Graves joined the Royal Navy at an early age and rose steadily in rank and reputation; he was second in command to Lord Nelson on board the *Defiance* at the ferocious Battle of Copenhagen in 1801 and he was knighted on the quarterdeck of the *St George* by Lord Nelson for his bravery in this action. A fuller account of the career of Sir Thomas Graves is provided at Appendix D, including extracts from a letter written the day after the battle to his brother John, in which amidst his reflections on his recent ordeal he adds 'Give my love to my dear daughter. She has ever the most ardent prayers for her happiness'.

Thomas Graves married twice, firstly to Bridget, daughter of Philip Bacon of Bishop's Hall, Battisford, Suffolk, on 22 August 1771 at St Alphege, Greenwich, and by her had his only child, Mary, who was baptised at Honiton on 1 November 1772. Bridget died on Christmas Eve 1795 and Sir Thomas eventually remarried to a wife named Susanna; this marriage appears to have taken place on 21 July 1808 at St James, Bath, Susanna's former name being Blackwell.[83]

Land tax returns show Thomas Graves as the owner of Colwell Wood from 1798 until 1813, and for much of this period he is also shown as the occupier (meaning that there was no tenant); but the returns for 1800 and 1801 record Nath(aniel) Stocker as the occupier. As we have seen, it was Nathaniel Stocker who sold an oak tree to the church in 1815 when the roof was rebuilt, but we have no evidence that he was still 'occupying' Colwell Wood at that date; and whether he was employed by the Graves family as woodman, or rented the woodland for his own benefit, we do not know. Nathaniel, who was born in about 1764, continued to live in Offwell, and was buried there on 11

---

[82] J K Laughton, 'Graves, Sir Thomas (*c.*1747–1814), revised by J D Davies, *Oxford Dictionary of National Biography* (Oxford University Press, 2004).
[83] Somerset & Dorset Family History Society: Index to Somerset Marriages/*Findmypast*.

August 1839 aged 75. His widow was probably Ann Stocker of Offwell, who was buried aged 74 on 21 July 1840.[84]

James Northcote's portrait of Admiral Sir Thomas Graves, 1801/2. The ship in the background is the 'Defiance' in action at the Battle of Copenhagen; the urn is in memory of Sir Thomas's first wife.
© National Maritime Museum, Greenwich, London.

Sir Thomas Graves would have bought his property in Colwell to complement his estate at Woodbine Hill, but as a naval officer he would have appreciated the value of timber. Sir Thomas had built Woodbine Hill (now known as Combe Hill) in 1789; the house stands in a commanding position, as befits an admiral, above the village of Combe Raleigh.[85] His brother John lived nearby at Exeter and would have kept an eye upon his niece while Sir Thomas was at sea, as he was for much of his life. His acquisitions in Devon – both in Combe Raleigh and in Offwell – took place in the 1790s when he was not in active service, but during some of this time he was in France. His

---

[84] Parish registers of Offwell.
[85] Combe House was severely damaged by fire in 2009, and has been restored.

daughter Mary was baptised in Honiton in 1772 and so Sir Thomas had evidently set up a home here after his marriage. Mary was 23 when her mother died.

Woodbine Hill, later known as Combe Hill, Devon[86]

Colwell Wood Cottage was built in the early years of the nineteenth century. As we have seen in the previous chapter, a 'Plan of Colwell Wood' was drawn up for Thomas Graves; it is undated but may have accompanied the deed of 1798 by which he finally purchased the property. No cottage is marked on this map, but there are pencil markings suggesting that someone was planning the development of the wood, perhaps including three ponds and a clearing. The site which appears to be marked out for a clearing represents the site of Colwell Wood Cottage, which was built by the time the first edition Ordnance Survey one-inch map was surveyed in 1806: it can just be seen in the west of the woodland area.

---

[86] Reproduced by permission of Historic England.

Surveyor's drawing of Colwell Wood for the One-Inch Ordnance Survey map of 1809 (surveyed 1806 by Robert Searle).[87] *This is the earliest evidence of the existence of Colwell Wood Cottage.*

It was in 1805, nine years before his death (and prior to his second marriage) that Admiral Graves made over Colwell Wood, together with his estates in Combe Raleigh, to his daughter Mary Graves, although this may have been a simple formality: the transaction was made 'for five shillings and out of love and affection'. As with the earlier conveyance, the transaction of 1805 was carried out in the form of a lease and release, and both documents are held among the Kinglake and Newman family papers which have been deposited on loan at the Somerset Heritage Centre:[88] The sale was effected on 3 and 4 December 1805 and the wood was described in the release as:

> a piece of woodland commonly called Colwell Wood situate in parish of Orfield [*sic*] near Honiton, now in possession of John Lathy as tenant, with outhouses, edifices, barns, stables, courts, meadows, timber etc.

No mention was made of a dwelling house there, but this is not conclusive. Curiously, the deed described Colwell as being in the parish of 'Orfield' or 'Urfield', which was clearly an error; this possibly indicates how insignificant the property was to Sir Thomas. At this point the tenant of Colwell Wood was one John Lathy, who had presumably succeeded Nathaniel Stocker. John

---

[87] © The British Library Board, OSD 45 pt.1, item 5.
[88] Kinglake and Newman Family Papers, Somerset Heritage Centre (South West Heritage Trust) DD\AY/349: see abstract at Appendix B, pages 101–101.

Lathy's name does not appear on the land tax returns but a John Lathy of Honiton left a will that was proved in 1825, the executor being Esther Lathy.[89]

We may therefore speculate that it was Mary who was responsible for building Colwell Wood Cottage, perhaps as a picturesque rural retreat, or perhaps for a more prosaic reason: to provide a residence for a woodman. War with France was still raging, and timber prices were high, so woodland was worth serious investment.

However, another explanation would be that having acquired a piece of land, Sir Thomas or his advisers decided that the addition of a dwelling house would increase its value, whatever the function of the property. Whatever the reason, building the house, and bringing the surrounding land under cultivation, would not have been particularly easy.

Having made over all his property to his only child in 1805, Sir Thomas Graves saw no need to make a will, and he died on 28 March 1814, intestate, at Woodbine Hill. Letters of administration were granted to his daughter Mary on 2 August 1815, his widow Susanna having renounced her right to act as administrator of his personal estate, which was worth about £1,500.

Mary raised a memorial to her parents in Combe Raleigh Church:

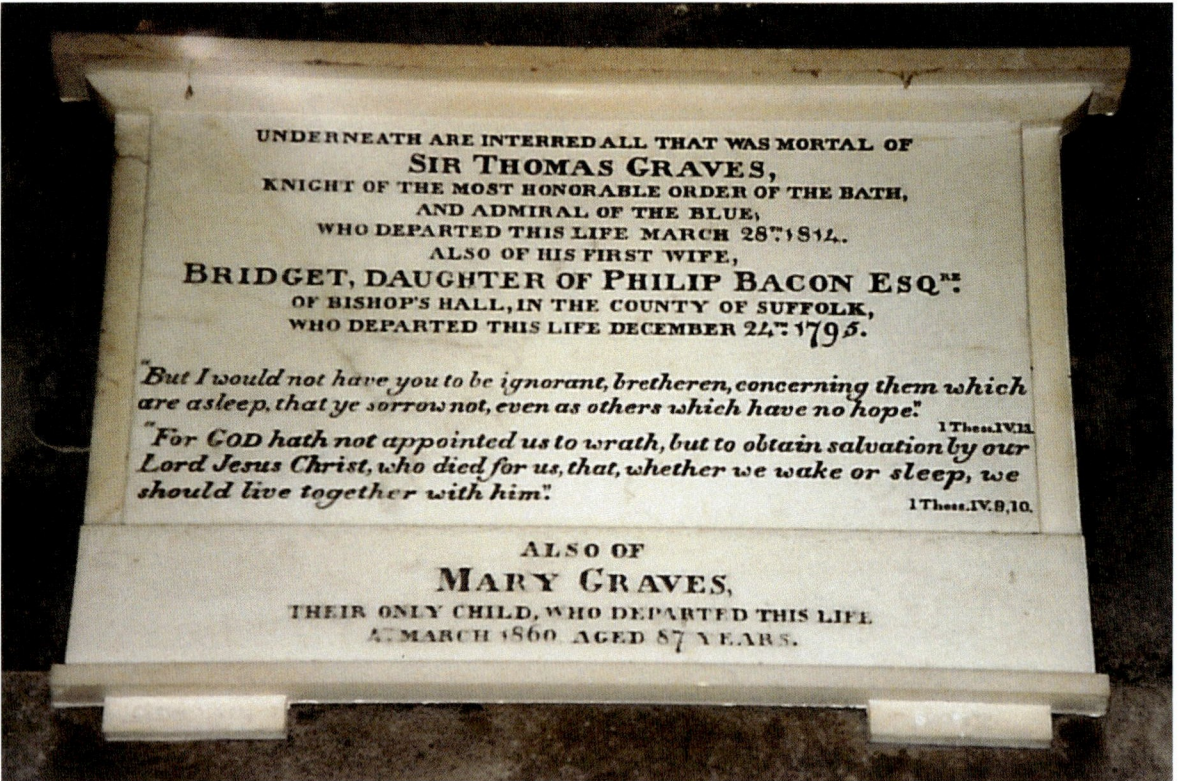

The Graves memorial, Combe Raleigh Church

---

[89] The National Archives, Estate Duty Register, IR 27/194. The will itself does not survive.

UNDERNEATH ARE INTERRED ALL THAT WAS MORTAL OF
SIR THOMAS GRAVES,
KNIGHT OF THE MOST HONOURABLE ORDER OF THE BATH
AND ADMIRAL OF THE BLUE
WHO DEPARTED THIS LIFE MARCH 28TH 1814
ALSO OF HIS FIRST WIFE
BRIDGET DAUGHTER OF PHILIP BACON ESQRE
OF BISHOP'S HALL, IN THE COUNTY OF SUFFOLK
WHO DEPARTED THIS LIFE DECEMBER 24TH 1795

"But I would not have you to be ignorant, bretheren, concerning them which are asleep, that ye
sorrow not, even as others which have no hope."
"For God hath not appointed us to wrath, but to obtain salvation by our Lord Jesus Christ, who died
for us, that, whether we wake or sleep, we should live together with him."

A year later, Mary's stepmother Susanna also died, at York Buildings, near Charing Cross in London. Her death was recorded in the *Gentleman's Magazine* in 1816:

In York-buildings, Lady Graves, widow of the late Adm. Sir Thos. Graves, K.B.

Mary Graves and her Tenants

In 1815, the year after her father's death, Mary Graves appears on the church rate list for Offwell as both owner and occupier of Colwell Wood, for which she paid 1s 9d, as her father had done ten years earlier. She made the same payment in the year 1821. The term 'occupier' does not denote residence, but there are some indications that Miss Graves took a personal interest in the wood and may have regarded it as of recreational as well as business value.

Land tax returns indicate that John Braddick was the occupier of Colwell Wood between 1822 and 1826. Although his burial entry is not found in the parish registers of Offwell, he probably died in 1826, for a 'Mrs Braddick' was paying church rates for the wood in 1829. The Braddicks were succeeded in the land tax returns for 1829 by 'Mr Burton'. Parish rate lists for Offwell for this period show John Braddick and Mr Burton being assessed as follows:

1824	John Bradick for Colwell Wood, occupier: 8¾d for poor rate; 1s 6¾d for church rate	
1825	John Braddick for Colwell Wood: 1s 6¾d	
1826	Jn Braddick for Colwell Wood	
1829	Mrs Braddic [*sic*] for Colwell Wood: 1s 6¾d	
1833	— Burton for Colwell Wood: 1s 6d for poor rate, 11s 8d for church rate[90]	

---

[90] Churchwardens' accounts, Offwell: Devon Archives 364A/PW3.

The church rate list for 1815 shows 'John Bradick' as the occupier of 'Sarles & Rouses', which were then the property of Mr Pounsford. He is probably the man who appears in the parish registers of Offwell in 1816 described as a husbandman:

Baptism
9 Jun 1816   Elizabeth daughter of John and Susannah Braddick [of] Offwell, husbandman, born 12 May

John Braddick and Susannah (Dunster) married at Offwell on 16 April 1811. However, there was another John Braddick in the parish who married Lucy Wench on 30 March 1815 (the witnesses being Philip Mitchell and William Braddick). The identity of '– Burton' (1833) is unclear but it is possible that this refers to John Burton of Honiton, whose burial was recorded in the parish registers of Offwell on 13 November 1843, aged 59.

In 1822 Samuel and Daniel Lysons' survey *Magna Britannica*[91] mentions a coppice-wood of about 100 acres in Offwell. By this time, the parish had been enclosed, the enclosure divisions being 'hedges well wooded', and again the most flourishing trees were oak and ash. Enclosure meant the appropriation of common ground for private use, and the rationalisation of small private holdings into larger ones, often to the detriment of the smallholders.

By this date, woodlands had acquired a value that was quite unconnected with their economic worth. Before the eighteenth century, when nature began to be seen as something for men to control and fashion at will, forests and woodlands were often treated with some trepidation; somewhere full of danger and mystery. During the romantic age, they assumed a more benign image: somewhere to admire the majestic beauty of nature and – for those who had any – a place in which to enjoy leisure. In 1798 William Wordsworth entreated his sister to:

Put on with speed your woodland dress;
And bring no book: for this one day
We'll give to idleness.[92]

Offwell's most famous son was Edward Copleston, Bishop of Llandaff (born 1776, died 1849), who was rector there as a young man between 1800 and 1804; thereafter, promotions and higher callings within the church meant that he was able to return to his home parish only occasionally, but family members continued to serve there as rectors until the 1950s, and were major landowners and benefactors in the parish. However, there can be no doubt about his great affection for Offwell, and particularly for its woods. He was educated at home in Offwell by his father until the age of 15, and his happy childhood memories were described in a letter dated 22 November 1825 to his friend John Duncan:

---

[91] Volume 6, page 374.
[92] 'To My Sister' (1798).

Bluebells in Colwell Wood, 2009

Natural history is the food of my vacation hours, and I shall take your precious volume with me when I next go to saunter and ramble in my Offwell woods. It would do my heart good to have you one day to join me in those rambles over the scenes of my infancy ...

In another letter, written just before he died to his friend Bruce Pryce, he described Offwell as his favourite retreat from the world, with its walks, rhododendrons and the 'old labourers' with whom he loved to converse.

The Bishop had long been keen to purchase woodland in Offwell; his nephew's *Memoir of Edward Copleston*[93] referred to his deep love of its 'steep green slopes, wooded dells, and clear brooks', and:

With these tastes and feelings, the bishop had cherished the hope, in his very early life, that he might one day possess for himself, and mould to his own fancy, the woodlands in which he had roamed and mused as a boy. These woodlands, together with some adjacent farms, did become his own in the course of years ...

Edward Copleston, Bishop of Llandaff (1776–1849): portrait by Thomas Phillips (1770–1845)[94]

The phrase 'mould to his own fancy' was significant, for the Bishop made it clear that woodland had to be tamed to be acceptable:

My chief boast is, that I have converted a squalid, unsightly, impassable dell into an agreeable range for pedestrians of all tastes: the domestic stroller, the contemplative lover of nature, the planter, the naturalist, even the sportsman, may enjoy a little recreation in this valley, which was once an impervious morass. It holds out to me the hope also of continual improvement, and I cannot but entertain a wish that my excellent poetical friend may hit off a few lines on the spot, which may be perpetuated on some rustic tablet.[95]

---

[93] William James Copleston, *Memoir of Edward Copleston, DD, Bishop of Llandaff* (London, 1851), page 106.

[94] Reproduced by permission of Amgueddfa Cymru - National Museum of Wales.

[95] *Ibid,* page 107: letter to John Duncan, 22 November 1825.

Although the Cottage and Colwell Wood were clearly let to tenants for much of her period of ownership, Mary Graves may have used them in the same Romantic spirit from time to time for her own enjoyment. The parish rate book for the year 1839 again lists her as both owner and occupier:

> 1839
> Mary Graves, Owner and Occupier of Colwell Wood, House and Coppice
> Rental: £30
> Rateable value: £20
> Rates: 2s 1d

Mary Graves was also assessed for a smaller property under the same name, with a gross estimated rental of £2 and rateable value of £1. The wood was described as 'coppice' at this date. The parish rate books for 1843 and 1844 give similar entries:

> 1843 and 4 March 1844
> Mary Graves, Owner and Occupier of House and Coppice: Colwell Wood
> Gross estimated rental: £32
> Rateable value: £21
> Church Rates: 2s 2¼d
> Rate: 5¼d[96]

There are two large-scale maps of Colwell from this period. The first, attached to the conveyance relating to the sale of Colwell Wood in January 1874,[97] is a coloured plan that was drawn up in 1838 (see below, page 58). This plan, which is entitled 'Colwell Wood, the property of Miss Mary Graves', clearly shows the 'Cottage and Garden', and adjoining them are small plots on which potatoes and barley were grown. Otherwise, Colwell Wood consisted of timber at various stages of growth; the largest plot was 13 acres in the northern part of Colwell Wood, which had 14 years' growth, and was thus planted in about 1824. In all, the property amounted to just over 45 acres.

It is interesting to note that this is the earliest map to show the carriageway (or 'loop') through the woods; this was constructed to avoid the steep gradient of the bridleway, which went more directly from the road at the north-west corner of Colwell Wood down to the Cottage. The new carriageway was mentioned in the Offwell parish vestry minute book on 24 March 1885 as '... the newer and more level but circuitous wheeltrack made by Mrs Graves ...'.[98]

We may speculate that Mary Graves used the Cottage for summer parties and recreation, although the plots of potatoes and barley indicate that its principal function, by 1838 at least, was a more prosaic one.

---

[96] Churchwardens' accounts, Offwell: Devon Archives 364A/PW3.

[97] Somerset Heritage Centre (South West Heritage Trust) DD\AY/349/1–5. The older map is annotated with pencil marks in preparation for the revised (pink) map which accompanied the deed of sale of 1874.

[98] The title 'Mrs' was not restricted to married women at this period.

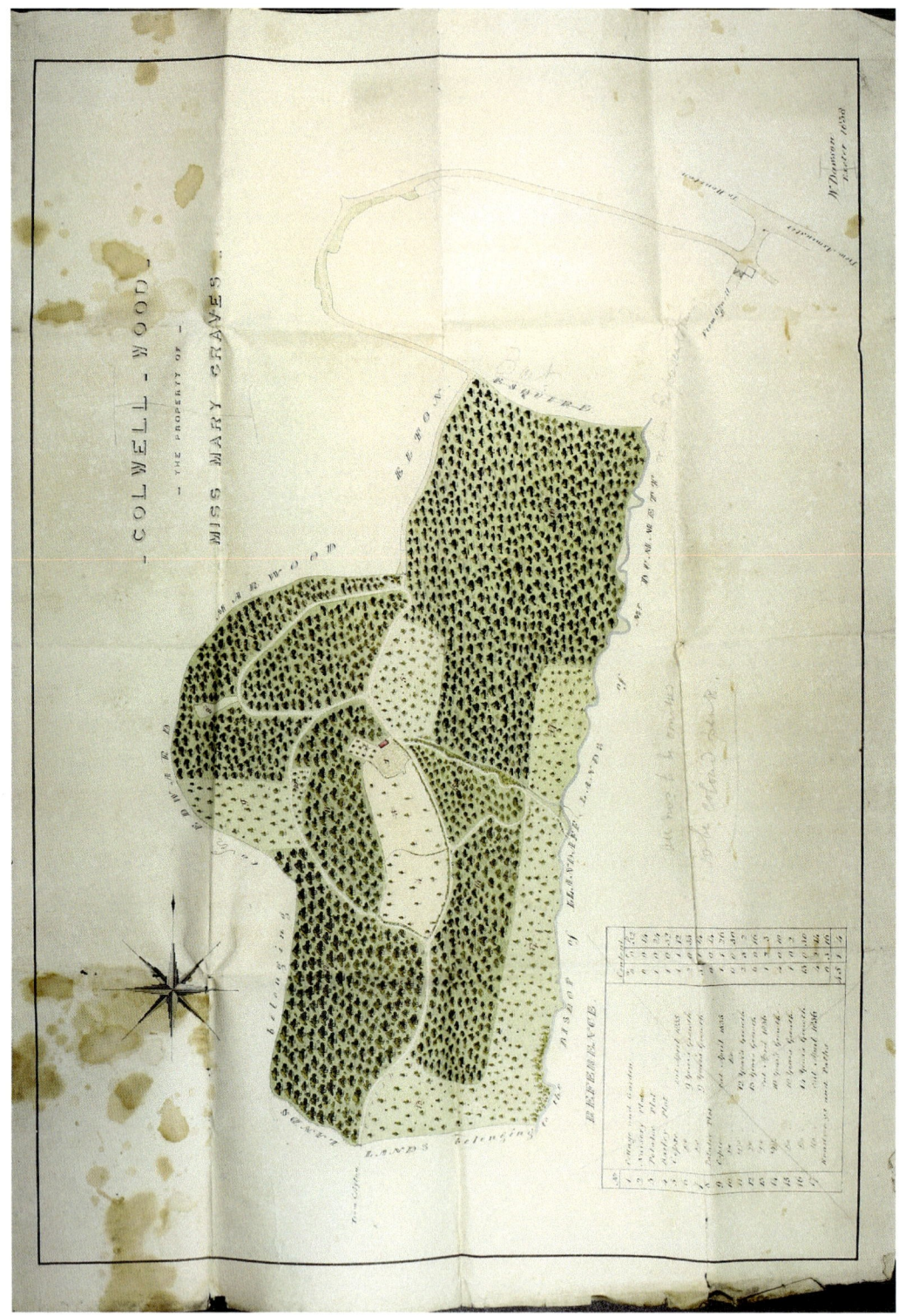

The Colwell Wood Estate in 1838[99]

[99] Kinglake and Newman Family Papers, Somerset Heritage Centre (South West Heritage Trust) DD\AY/349/6.

Key to Colwell Wood Estate Plan (1838)

Secondly, there is the Tithe Award and Map of 1842–45.[100] The Tithe Commutation Act of 1836 rationalised the process of commuting tithes owed to the Church and clergy, a system that went back to the middle ages. Instead of paying tithes in kind (such as a tenth of all produce), landowners made cash payments. The 1836 Act authorised commissioners to negotiate cash settlements on a professional valuation of the land, and hence large-scale maps were drawn up, with accompanying schedules showing the ownership and occupancy of land.

The Tithe Award and Map for Offwell shows Mary Graves owning and occupying Great Colwell Wood (plot 293), which is described as furze, comprising just over 39 acres, together with two much smaller areas of waste land (plots 287 and 288), one of them called Willow Bed. Colwell Wood Cottage, however, is listed as 'Cottage Gardens and yard' (plot 291), comprising under an acre and in the occupation of James Cox, together with other small plots of pasture nearby:

---

[100] Devon Archives 364A/PB 1–2. Award 1842, confirmed 1845. Map 1843.

Section of Offwell Tithe Map, 1843, showing plots owned by Mary Graves[101]

Apportionment of the Rent-charge in lieu of Tithes in Parish of Offwell, Devon
26 October 1842

Plot No	Landowner	Occupier	Description and name	State of cultivation	Extent	Rent charge apportioned
287	Mary Graves	Herself	Willow Bed	Waste	3r 21p	3d
288	Mary Graves	Herself		Waste	3r 21p	2d
289	Mary Graves	James Cox		Pasture	1a 24p	1s 2d
290	Mary Graves	James Cox		Waste	1a	10d
291	Mary Graves	James Cox	Cottage, garden & yard		1r 8p	1s
292	Mary Graves	James Cox	Little Plot	Pasture	22p	1d
293	Mary Graves	Herself	Great Colwell Wood	Furze	39a 2r 8p	£2 10s

---

[101] Devon Archives DEX/4/a/TM/Offwell. Reproduced with the kind permission of Devon Archives and Local Studies Service.

Overall, the parish of Offwell amounted to 1,918 acres, of which 127 were classified as woodland and 345 as furze land and waste.

The Cox Family

Who then was James Cox, the first known occupant of Colwell Wood Cottage? The name Cox appears in church rate lists at this period in relation to other small properties in Offwell, and in the 1773 list there was a property called 'Coxes or the Old Inn' which had become, by 1795, just 'Coxes'. The parish registers confirm that the Coxes were a well-established family in Offwell: James and Mary Cox had children James and John baptised there on 5 November 1815 and 22 March 1818 respectively. James, who was described as a husbandman in the baptism register, was buried there on 23 February 1860 at the impressive age of 86. There is no evidence that James Cox was a woodsman as such.

From 1841 onwards we have the benefit of decennial census returns, which give an interesting 'snapshot' of the occupants of Colwell Wood Cottage from 1841 to 1901, and our first real evidence of who was actually living there. In 1841 John Cox, who was aged between 60 and 64 and was defined as a yeoman, lived at 'Colwell Wood' with Lydia Cox, presumably his wife, who was aged between 55 and 59. We do not know what relationship John had to James Cox, who was Mary Graves' tenant in 1842, but the 1841 census shows James Cox living nearby at 'White Down' with his wife Mary and son James, and the two men might have perhaps been brothers or cousins:

Census 6 June 1841
TNA HO 107 214 book 14 fol 8 page 11
Colwell Wood, Offwell

		Occupation	*Whether born in county*
John Cox	60	Yeoman	N
Lydia *D[itt]o*	55		N
Philip Bagwell	12	M[ale] S[ervant]	Y

White Down

		Occupation	*Whether born in county*
James Cox	65	Ag Lab	No
Mary *D[itt]o*	50		Y
James *Do*	20	Thatcher	Y

Neither John nor his wife Lydia was born in Devon. They had one young boy servant, Philip Bagwell, aged 12. The fact that John was a yeoman (a slightly vague term at this date, but one that usually described someone who farmed his own land), and employed a servant, shows that the status of the Cottage still at a height; from this point it probably descended gradually into disrepair throughout the century.

In this same year, Mary Graves was recorded in the census living at Woodbine Hill, Combe Raleigh, with a relatively modest staff of three servants.[102]

James and Mary Cox were still living in Offwell in 1851[103] but James was now very elderly (78) and described as a pauper. Their address was not given but the next household was White Cross Cottage. This record reveals that James came from the parish of Lillington ('Lilenton') in Dorset, and we may guess that this too was where John Cox of Colwell Wood Cottage came from.

The Samson Family

In 1851, John Samson, an agricultural labourer, lived in the Cottage with his wife Elizabeth and their two young children, Edwin aged three and John aged one. Elizabeth and the children were born in Stockland and John was born in Cotleigh; there was also a young visitor, Mary Pike, aged 11:

Census 30 March 1851
TNA HO 107 1863 fol 88 page 4
Schedule No 18: Colwell Wood Cot[tage], Offwell

				Occupation	*Where born*
John Samson	Head	Mar	28	Ag Labourer	[Devon] Cotleigh
Elizabeth Samson	Wife	Mar	25		*Do* Stockland
Edwin Samson	Son		5	At Home	*Do* Stockland
John Samson	Son		1	*Do*	*Do* Stockland
Mary Pike	Visitor		11		*Do* Stockland

Two months after this census was taken, John and Elizabeth Samson (the surname was recorded on this occasion as Sansom) presented another child, Elizabeth, for baptism in Offwell church, followed by three younger children, which probably explains why they left the Cottage, hopefully for more spacious accommodation, before the time of the next census:

Baptisms
30 May 1852   Elizabeth daughter of John & Elizabeth Sansom of Offwell, labourer
5 Mar 1854   William son of John and Elizabeth Sansom of Offwell, labourer
2 Sep 1860   Edwin son of John and Elizabeth Sansom of Offwell, labourer
9 Apr 1865   Ellen daughter of John and Elizabeth Sansom of Offwell, labourer

It is very likely that the two eldest children, Elizabeth and William, were born at Colwell Wood Cottage, but unfortunately the parish register does not give their exact address within the parish.

---

[102] The National Archives HO 107 200, book 18, fol 6, page 7.
[103] The National Archives HO 107 1863 fol 87 page 2.

CHAPTER FOUR: THE NINETEENTH CENTURY

Death and Will of Mary Graves

Mary Graves died, of 'paralysis and low fever', at Woodbine Hill on 4 March 1860, aged 87, shortly after the death of her equally elderly former tenant, James Cox. She had made her will, which runs to 19 pages, on 30 November 1852, with two codicils dated February 1853 and November 1855. The will was proved on 23 March 1860. She requested a simple burial and memorial in Combe Raleigh church, where she had already provided a blank space on a tablet above her parents' grave:

> I desire that my funeral may be conducted with simplicity and that my remains shall not be conveyed in a Hearse but shall be borne to my Parish Church on the shoulders of as many of the most sober and respectable Labourers as shall be necessary resident either in the above Parish of Combe Raleigh or in that of Dunkeswell...

> The following words shall be inscribed on the space left on the Mural Tablet erected by me above my Parents Grave or Vault in the Parish Church of Combe Raleigh namely 'Also of Mary Graves their only child who departed this life...'

Mary left the portrait of her father by Northcote to her cousin Sir Joseph Sawle Graves Sawle, baronet. This is a three-quarter length oil painting (shown above, page 49) dated 1801/2; the artist, James Northcote (1746–1831), was a follower of Joshua Reynolds. The subject is shown in rear-admiral's dress uniform, exhibiting the star of the Knight Bachelor. A large funerary urn shares the foreground with Sir Thomas, on the plinth of which are the words:

> SACRED TO THE
> MEMORY
> OF BRIDGET, THE WIFE OF
> REAR ADM.
> SIR THO.S GRAVES K.B.
> OF WOODBINE-HILL IN THE COUNTY OF
> DEVON,
> AND DAUGHTER OF
> PHILIP BACON ESQ.
> OF BISHOPS HALL IN THE
> COUNTY OF SUFFOLK,
> WHO DEPARTED THIS LIFE
> THE 24.TH OF DECEMBER
> 1795

In the background is a depiction of the *Defiance* in action at the Battle of Copenhagen. Mary asked her cousin to keep the portrait or to place it in the Gallery of Naval Officers in Greenwich Hospital, in return for a copy already presented to King William IV by Sir Joseph. In 1989 it was noted that the picture had been moved to 10 Downing Street to hang in the place of Romney's *Lady in Blue* (see Appendix D, page 120) but it is now back at the National Maritime Museum at Greenwich.

Mary Graves also left Sir Joseph another picture of his choice from Woodbine Hill, and a wax model of her father 'done by Mr Rowe'. In addition to Woodbine Hill, her freehold property included land in the adjoining parish of Dunkeswell, and she also owned the advowson of Dunkeswell. Her real estate at Dunkeswell (not the advowson) was placed in trust[104] for the benefit of the children of her deceased cousin Mary Anne, wife of Revd Cremer Cremer of Milton, Norfolk; Maria wife of the trustee Revd John Billington; Sophia wife of Revd Charles Barnwell, rector of Milcham, Norfolk; and Arabella, widow of Revd George Whitefoord. The advowson was left to another clergyman, Revd Henry Addington Simcoe of Penheale, Cornwall.

The Simcoes were a gentry family of Wolford Lodge in Dunkeswell, where Mary had evidently acquired land in addition to that which her father had given her. Mary's funeral arrangements were placed in the hands of Mrs Anne Pring of Ivedon, Awliscombe and of 'one of my dear friends of the Simcoe family resident at Wolford Lodge'.

The remainder of Mary's real estate was initially placed in a separate trust[105] for the use of her cousin John Samuel Graves for his lifetime, and then to his eldest son, Thomas Molyneux Graves.

The numerous personal bequests made by Mary in her will provide some insights into her long life. Her belongings included a collection of minerals, shells and medals, which she left to Maria, wife of John Samuel Graves; to her principal beneficiary John Samuel Graves she left a miniature of her father by 'Mr Leaky.' John Samuel's son, George Samuel Graves, received her 'chronometer by Earnshawe'. Mary had something of a romantic streak, and to her coachman and her other domestic servants she left 'as many sovereigns as they shall have had years in my service'. Other beneficiaries were friends, and her belongings included:

> a little gold watch
> a shell and silver snuff box
> a painting in oil of Lord Nelson
> a large diamond ring
> a small diamond ring with my father's hair
> my lace and wearing apparel

Mary did not forget her tenants, and requested that seven-year leases should be immediately issued to her tenants in Combe Raleigh and Dunkeswell.

In the second codicil, she bequeathed her 'freehold tenements situate or arising within the Parish of Offwell and Honiton …' to her cousin, John Samuel Graves, absolutely and without any restriction; in other words it was not to be held by trustees and John Samuel could dispose of it as he wished. As mentioned above, he was also permitted to have a copy of the Northcote portrait of Sir Thomas Graves. Finally, he was appointed executor of her will.

---

[104] The trustees for the Dunkeswell estate were Mary's cousin Livingston Thompson of Dublin, Revd John Billington and John Bridgeman Smith, solicitor of Honiton.
[105] The trustees for this were Mary's cousin John Samuel Graves, Livingston Thompson and John Billington.

THE GRAVES FAMILY

Owners of Colwell Wood are underlined

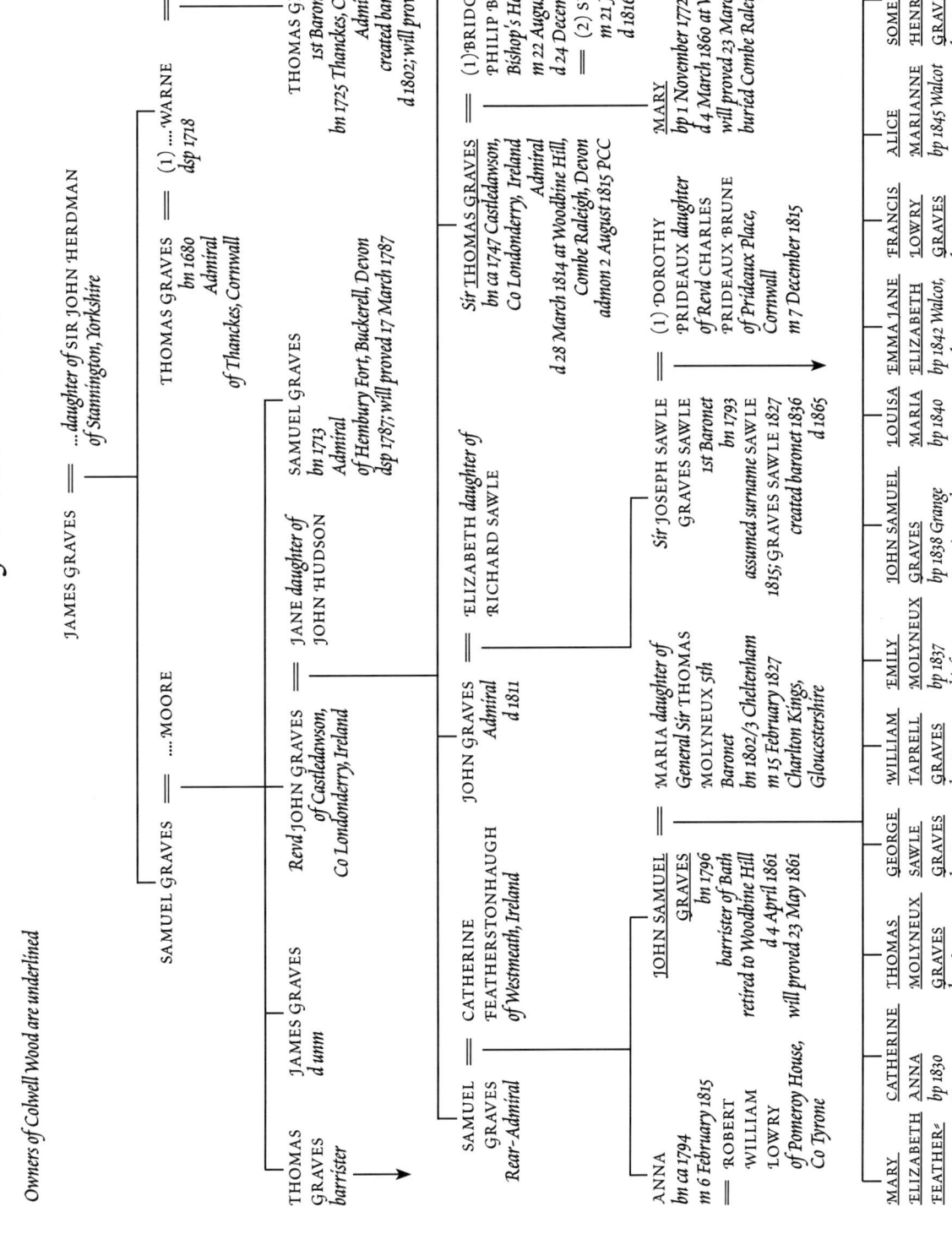

The Kinglake and Newman family papers include two documents relating to the estate duty payable on Mary Graves' estate.[106] We learn from one of these documents that in 1860 her cottage and woods in Colwell yielded a gross annual rent of £25; this is comparable to the estimate made in 1839 of the gross rental as £30 and confirms that the status of the property had been in something of a decline since the days of James Cox.

John Samuel Graves and his Tenants

John Samuel Graves, the heir to Mary's estate of Colwell Wood, was born in 1796, the son of Admiral Sir Thomas Graves' eldest brother Samuel. John Samuel was a barrister who lived at 15 Burlington Street, Bath, before retiring to Woodbine Hill after his cousin's death. His tenure of his cousin's estate was brief, since he died on 4 April 1861, just over a year after Mary's own death.

By coincidence, the 1861 census was taken the day after the death of John Samuel Graves. This showed that the Cottage in Colwell Wood was occupied by Richard Mitchell and his family. Richard was a butcher, then aged 48; his wife Mary was a year younger and worked as a charwoman; their children were Harriet aged 15, Charlotte aged 10, who both worked as servants, and Richard Mitchell junior aged 10 who was at school. All members of the family were born in Offwell:

Census 7 April 1861
TNA RG 9 1375 fol 74 page 12
Schedule No 61: Colwell Wood, Offwell

				Occupation	*Where born*	
Richard Mitchell	Head	Mar	48	Butcher	[Devon, Offwell]	
Mary *Do*	Wife	Mar	47	Charwoman	*Do*	*Do*
Harriet *Do*	Daur	Un	15	Servant	*Do*	*Do*
Charlotte *Do*	Daur	Un	10	*Do*	*Do*	*Do*
Richard *Do*	Son		7	Scholar	*Do*	*Do*

Ten years later, when the 1871 census was taken, Richard and Mary Mitchell were still living at the Cottage; Richard was now described as a farmer and Mary as a laundress. Only their younger daughter, Charlotte, who was also described as a laundress, was still living with them. By the time the 1881 census was taken, the Mitchell family had moved away, and the Cottage in Colwell Wood was unoccupied.

The Mitchells had not gone far: they were living in Talaton, a few miles west of Honiton, and living in a laundry, probably on the estate of Escot House. Richard, Mary and their daughter Eliza were all now described as laundry workers and they had a servant, a young deaf girl called Elizabeth Sturries.

---

[106] Somerset Heritage Centre (South West Heritage Trust) DD\AY/349.

The Heirs of John Samuel Graves

John Samuel Graves and his wife, Maria, who were married on 15 February 1827 at Charlton Kings, just outside Cheltenham, Gloucestershire, had 14 children. The eldest, Lieutenant Thomas Molyneux Graves of the Royal Engineers, was killed at the assault on the Redan in the Crimean War on 18 June 1855, aged 24; there is a memorial to him in Combe Raleigh church (see below). A younger daughter, Emily Molyneux Graves (born in 1837), also died young.

John Samuel Graves made his will, which was brief and somewhat informal, on 4 June 1860, not long after inheriting his cousin's estates; this did not mention his property in Colwell, but all the surviving children were equal beneficiaries of their father's estate, apart from Woodbine Hill, which Mary Graves had already willed to Thomas Molyneux Graves, John Samuel's eldest son. An abstract is shown at Appendix C (page 117). The testator appointed his wife Maria and his son George Sawle Graves as executors and he devised to them his entire estate in trust 'for all my children except that son to whom Woodbine Hill has been devised by my cousin's will'. The will was proved on 23 May 1861. The effects were originally valued at under £4,000 but this was evidently too conservative an estimate, for the will was re-sworn at the Stamp Office in October 1863, the effects being then valued rather more highly at under £7,000.

Memorial to Thomas Molyneux Graves in Combe Raleigh Church

Thus from May 1861 Colwell Wood was owned jointly by the twelve surviving Graves siblings. Their number was reduced to eleven in 1872 with the death of John Samuel junior. Such a large number of joint owners cannot have been entirely satisfactory, and in 1874 it was decided to sell the property to their neighbour Sir Edward Marwood-Elton.

The deed of sale and transfer of Colwell Wood, which was dated 9 January 1874, was accompanied by two depositions, which set out full personal details of the Graves vendors.[107] John Samuel's widow, Maria, who went to live in Lyme Regis, Dorset, after her husband's death, was also a party to the transaction. The first deposition was by John Samuel Graves' son George Sawle Graves, Commander, RN, of Lyme Regis, Dorset: it stated that his father had inherited Colwell Wood from his cousin Mary Graves. George listed his siblings with their dates of baptism:

(i & ii)   Mary Elizabeth Fetherstonaugh Graves and Catherine Anna Graves, baptised 14 Nov 1830 at Tormarton, Gloucestershire.

(iii)   Thomas Molyneux Graves baptised 17 September 1831 at St Martin in the Fields, London. Bachelor. Died 18 June 1855 in the Crimea.

(iv)   Myself, baptised at Tormarton on 4 November 1832.

(v)   William Taprell Graves baptised 2 April 1835 at Grange, Co Armagh, Ireland.

(vi)   Emily Molyneux Graves baptised 12 February 1837 at Grange. Died an infant.

(vii)   John Samuel Graves baptised 7 October 1838 at Grange. Died 1872.

(viii)   Louisa Maria Graves baptised 28 June 1840 at Grange.

(ix)   Emma Jane Elizabeth Graves (now wife of Frederick William Wetherell) baptised 11 January 1842 at Walcot, Bath.

(x)   Francis Lowry Graves baptised 6 December 1843 at Walcot.

(xi)   Alice Marianne Graves baptised on 23 October 1845 at Walcot.

(xii)   Somerset Henry Paul Graves baptised 23 April 1847 at Walcot.

(xiii)   Isabel Graves baptised 28 July 1848 at Walcot.

(xiv)   Constance Mary Graves baptised 8 April 1853 at Walcot.

The second deposition was by John Samuel Graves' sister Anna Lowry, now a widow of Belmore in County Westmeath, Ireland. She stated that her brother had married Maria on 15 February 1827 at Charlton Kings, Gloucestershire, and repeated the information regarding his children.

The deed of sale itself is partially decayed and some of the text is lost. The property was described:

All that estate or piece and parcel of woodland (on part whereof a cottage has been erected and other parts have been brought under cultivation) commonly called Colwell Wood situate lying and being in the parish of Offwell in the said County of Devon formerly the estate of John Mayne of the City of Exeter deceased, afterwards of John Mayne of Kensington in the County of Middlesex, deceased, then of Thomas Mayne of Enfield in the said county of Middlesex, deceased, since of Thomas Graves deceased, then of Mary Graves deceased and late of the said John Samuel Graves the testator, deceased, all which hereditaments and premises are by way of further description but not so as to bridge the grant and conveyance thereof hereinbefore made more particularly described and delineated in the plan drawn on the back of the second skin of

---

[107] Somerset Heritage Centre (South West Heritage Trust) DD\AY/349: see abstract at Appendix B.

these presents and whereon the same are colored pink. Together with all buildings commons timber and other trees underwoods fences hedges ditches wastes ways paths passages waters watercourses liberties privileges easements rights members and appurtenances whatsoever …

Part of the 1874 conveyance, with thirteen signatures and seals (Somerset Heritage Centre DD\AY/349)

The price was £1,500, which was divided among the eleven surviving children, each of whom received £136 7s 6d. Each of the children[108] signed for their portion (as did Emma Jane's husband) and their endorsements are shown at the foot of the deed, together with that of their mother.

On the reverse of this last document, which is a large parchment sheet, there is a coloured map of the property (see below), which was based on the 1838 map.

---

[108] William Taprell Graves' endorsement shows the signature of his attorney: all the others signed themselves.

Plan of Colwell Wood, from the 1874 Conveyance (Somerset Heritage Centre DD\AY/349)

Neither the 1798 deed, nor the 1874 deed of sale, specifies the precise acreage of the property. In the latter deed it was noted that a cottage had been erected on the estate and that 'other parts have been brought under cultivation'.

Thus in 1874 Colwell Cottage and Wood entered a new phase in their history, being now annexed to the Widworthy estate, and the property of the Marwood-Elton family.

Chapter Five
THE MARWOOD-ELTON ERA (1874–1937)

Sir Edward Marwood-Elton

The purchaser of Colwell Wood from the Graves family in 1874 was Sir Edward Marwood-Elton, builder of Widworthy Court, a striking Victorian mansion that lies just over the parish boundary, to the east of Colwell Wood. As mentioned in Chapter Three, the Marwoods were established among the gentry of Devon from at least the sixteenth century, and at some point between 1725 and 1734, Thomas Marwood (died 1748) had purchased a large portion of the manor of Colwell, although this did not include Colwell Wood. His descendant Sir Edward Marwood-Elton was born in 1800, the son of James Marwood Elton (1776–1827), and the grandson of Frances Marwood (1749–1780) of Widworthy and her husband, Edward Elton (died 1811) of Bristol. The Marwood and Elton families had been united by the marriage of this couple in 1761. Sir Edward assumed 'Marwood' as additional surname by royal licence in 1830 and was created a baronet in 1838. He had an MA from Brasenose College, Oxford, and was a lawyer who ultimately became a Queen's Counsel. He was an important figure locally, being successively JP, High Sheriff and finally Deputy-Lieutenant for the county; he also served as MP for East Devon, but lost his seat after the Reform Bill of 1832.[109]

Widworthy Court

Sir Edward would have been very familiar with Colwell Wood, because twenty-five years earlier he had a serious dispute over two ornamental fish ponds that Bishop Edward Copleston had constructed in the grounds of Offwell House. We do not know exactly when the ponds were made; probably in the late 1830s and certainly by 1838 when D McNee Stirling described them:

---

[109] *Debrett's Illustrated Baronetage and Knightage* (1865); *Burke's Landed Gentry* (1952); Ramsden, *Parochial History*, Appendix, page 53.

In Colwell wood, which occupied an area of about a hundred acres, Bishop Coplestone has effected great and valuable improvements, which include the formation of capacious fish-ponds, and other artificial decorations, that prove highly ornamental to the place.[110]

For several years they were uncontroversial. The ponds were formed from a stream which ran from Colwell Wood through the Bishop's land and then ultimately into the lands of Sir Edward Marwood-Elton. They were formed by digging out each side of the Colwell Wood stream; they measured about 150–180 feet across, but were rather longer than they were wide. The stream passed through the ponds, and was one of three streams that fed Offwell Brook (or the 'Mill Leat'), which supplied Colwell Mill.

Old postcard of Colwell Wood Ponds, 'A pretty spot'

The freehold owner of the mill was Sir Edward Marwood-Elton and he leased it to his tenant, John Dare. For several years the miller John Dare made no complaint about the ponds, but shortly before 1848 he appears to have upgraded his mill from a grist mill to grinding higher quality flour for sale, and this meant that he required a larger flow of water from the stream. The Bishop and his lawyers claimed that building the ponds had no effect on the volume of water that flowed into the Mill Leat. However, in 1848 the Bishop drained off some of his land between the ponds, and to do this a channel was dug under the Mill Leat; it was this action that triggered the dispute. Dare claimed that his supply was now diminished and he therefore entered the Bishop's land and lifted the hatches which dammed the water to fill the lower pond. This led to correspondence between the Bishop and Sir Edward through their lawyers. Sir Edward demanded the right to draw water from the ponds,

---

[110] D McNee Stirling, *The Beauties of the Shore: A Guide to the Watering-Places of the South-East Coast of Devon* (1838).

particularly during hot, dry summers when evaporation caused the stream to diminish, but he had persuaded John Dare not to bring an action in the County Court. Bishop Copleston replied that he was quite prepared to authorise his steward to open the hatches in hot summers to increase the flow, but stated that any evaporation was minute. He was not prepared to allow Dare to act unilaterally in entering his property and opening the hatches without permission.

Neither side gave ground and on 26 March 1849 Dare opened the hatches without permission; Sir Edward supported him by claiming that he had every right to do so. The Bishop's steward, Henry Robinson, reacted angrily and according to Sir Edward 'has threatened personal violence', namely to throw anyone who opened the hatches into the water. This provoked Sir Edward, who lost his temper and personally went to the ponds and opened the hatches himself. He claimed he had every right to do this until the flow of water was restored, and he further claimed that the ponds seriously reduced the value of his property. Bishop Copleston was conciliatory and an inspection of the ponds and streams by the lawyers for both sides and Sir Edward's bailiff was held on 15 June 1849. The Bishop suggested that arbitrators should be appointed to measure the loss of water to the mill and to compensate Dare, but when Sir Edward refused to accept this, the Bishop said he would go to court, presumably to sue for trespass or to get an injunction prohibiting Dare and Sir Edward from entering his land. Meanwhile, the lawyers drew up an interim agreement, dated 14 July 1849, whereby until the dispute was resolved 'John Dare, occupier of Colwell Mills, property of Sir Edward Marwood Elton, shall be allowed to stop the water or turn it on to grind his corn, on giving notice to Henry Robinson, agent of the Bishop, but this turning on/off shall not be taken as evidence of any rights'.

Bishop Copleston died before he had initiated any court proceedings, and according to the Bishop's lawyers (Messrs Townsend & Stamp), Dare continued to act responsibly according to the interim agreement, so no further action was taken. However, nine years later, in 1858, the dispute flared up again, and the Bishop's executors claimed that recently Dare 'has constantly entered the grounds of Offwell House and broken the ponds, both the Higher and Lower one, by placing timber and sods to raise the levels of the pond by nearly a foot and then removing them'. The matter was again put into the hands of lawyers, and the Bishop's representative sought an 'opinion' from a barrister, J D Coleridge. This legal opinion set out the history of the ponds, and is our main source of information about the dispute.[111] The opinion also addressed the legal question of riperian rights, such as 'To what extent can interference be justified?'. Coleridge said that only one who has sustained actual injury can bring a legal action, and in this case it was a question of fact: 'Can Sir Edward Marwood-Elton show any diminution of flow, and damage to the miller's interest?'. So far as we know, the dispute was not taken any further, and hence the Offwell estate must have come to another informal agreement with Sir Edward and his tenant John Dare.

As we have mentioned above,[112] Bishop Copleston had purchased West Colwell from the Southcott family shortly before 1822. The church rate book for 1839 confirms this, showing that he was the owner of West Colwell, which brought him an annual rent of £48. West Colwell comprised over

---

[111] 'Miscellaneous letters to Bishop Copleston', Devon Archives 1149/F24: a brief sketch of the streams and mill is included with the 'Opinion'.

[112] See page 33.

130 acres in 1861, making it one of the larger farms in the parish. As we have just seen, Colwell Mills was owned by Sir Edward Marwood-Elton, as a part of the extensive Widworthy estate. Thus the fragmented pattern of ownership in Colwell continued throughout the nineteenth century.

Marwood-Elton Arms

Sir Edward Marwood-Elton was the first and last baronet; he died unmarried on 18 April 1884, and his three younger brothers had all been bachelors too and all had predeceased him. Under the terms of his will (dated 18 February 1882, proved 27 June 1884) his Widworthy estate, which included Colwell Wood, passed to Revd Alfred Elton, who was the son of his deceased cousin, Henry Edward Elton. In accordance with Sir Edward's will, Alfred assumed the arms and the additional surname Marwood by royal licence in 1885, and was thereafter Alfred Marwood-Elton of Widworthy Court. Although he was married, Alfred also died childless, on 20 April 1911.

The Stamp Family

Meanwhile, the Cottage in Colwell Wood is believed to have been occupied by the Stamp family in the early 1880s, although the 1881 census found it to be empty. William Stamp, born in about 1835 in Northleigh, Devon, married twice, firstly on 6 May 1855 at Farway to Ann Reed, by whom he had at least seven children (Mary A, Frank, Ella, Sarah, Mark, George and Alice). William's marriage certificate shows that he was the son of Gilbert Stamp, a labourer. Ann, who was the daughter of Thomas Reed, a labourer, died in 1877 at the age of 44.

William married secondly, on 12 September 1883 at Offwell, to Eliza Pratt, a servant,[113] by whom he had a further eight children, all of whom survived infancy, these being Gladys, Gilbert J, Beatrice Jane, Florie Kett, Jack, Harry, Tom (who was born on 19 February 1894 and died in 1971) and Dick.[114]

Census returns describe William Stamp as an agricultural labourer but in 1891 and 1901 he was not working for anyone else. At the time of the 1881 census he was living in Offwell, at Mount Pleasant, and he described himself as a road contractor. One of his grandsons, Bob Stamp, recalls that William rented two fields above the Cottage, and retained these even after he moved away; he described his grandfather as a 'husbandry man' and amateur vet. The 1891 census found William at Monkton.

The Stamp family had settled in Cotleigh, Devon, by 1906, when the children's section of the *Western Times* recorded that Tom Stamp, of 'Pigeon's Cottage', Cotleigh, was commended for a drawing entitled 'After a Day's Sport'.[115] Eliza Jane Stamp, widow of William, died at her son Tom's house there (by this time it was known rather more elegantly as 'Dovecot') in March 1939,

---

[113] In the section for 'Father's name and surname' the marriage certificate, very unusually, shows the words 'Incesto patre': Eliza was the child of an incestuous union between father and daughter.

[114] These details are from the 1861, 1871, 1881, 1891, 1901 and 1911 census returns and from the General Register Office indexes to births, marriages and deaths.

[115] *Western Times*, 12 April 1906, page 7.

aged 81, and it was the rector of Offwell, Edward Copleston, who officiated at her funeral in Cotleigh. Her obituary in the *Devon and Exeter Gazette* said that:

> She was much respected and assisted in social events, especially for the schoolchildren. She had been in failing health for some time. The funeral took place in Cotleigh Churchyard on Monday, amid every token of respect.[116]

Six of Eliza's eight children were among the mourners at the funeral.

Family tradition relates that Tom Stamp (born 1894) had a horse named Fan, and that he was charged with distilling illegal whiskey, but this has not been verified.[117] He received small prizes at several Honiton Shows from 1932 to 1939 for having been employed since Lady Day, 1911, by Mr S F Netherway of Hill's Farm, Cotleigh.[118]

A further clue to the occupants of the Cottage in the 1880s is that on 24 March 1885 a meeting of the Offwell Parish Council decided that the road through Colwell Wood 'past the Keeper's Cottage' was a parish road, while the 'new circuitous road to the Cottage' was a private road. This suggests that there was a gamekeeper to the Widworthy estate in residence in the Cottage at this date, as there was later, and this, as far as we know, was the first time that the property was thus used.

The Third Reform Act of 1884 greatly enlarged the electorate in country areas. Before this date there is no mention of any voter living in Colwell Wood in the electoral registers, no doubt because the occupants of the Cottage would not have been qualified to vote. In 1886 the electoral registers do not list Colwell Wood, but mention a dwelling house in Offwell Wood, occupied by Richard Miles; since there is no record of a dwelling in Offwell Wood, this may refer to Colwell Wood Cottage. Moreover, Richard Miles has been identified in the 1891 census as a gamekeeper. By this time he was living in the hamlet of Kiddon, Ashton, Devon, which was a detached portion of the parish of Exminster. He was born in Hampshire in 1855/6 and had a wife named Alice and seven children.[119] Gamekeepers often moved long distances from one job to another, and in 1881 Richard Miles was working at Llanina in Cardiganshire.[120]

The Dare Family

In 1890 Colwell Wood Cottage was temporarily occupied by the Dare family, who were prolific inhabitants of Offwell, being descended from William Dare, who was born in 1765 and was married twice, leaving numerous descendants.[121] William was the miller at Colwell Mill from the late eighteenth century, probably until his death in 1835. The Offwell church rate books show him as

---

[116] *Devon and Exeter Gazette,* 24 March 1939, page 2.

[117] Information on the Stamp family has been kindly supplied by Mr Bob Stamp.

[118] *Exeter and Plymouth Gazette,* 5 August 1932, page 5; *Exeter and Plymouth Gazette,* 11 August 1939.

[119] 1891 Census: The National Archives RG 12 1685 fol 43 page 49.

[120] 1881 Census: The National Archives RG 11 5441 fol 97 page 7.

[121] Information on the Dare family has been kindly supplied by Mrs Evelyn Sweetland, daughter of Thomas Edwin Dare.

the occupier of 'Colwell Mills and land' in 1833. The next rate list, made in 1839, shows his son John Dare, whom we have already encountered in the dispute over the Offwell ponds in the mid-nineteenth century, as the miller at Colwell Mill.

John's grandson, Thomas Edwin Dare, who was born in 1868, was gamekeeper to the Widworthy estate for nearly half a century, from 1886 until his death in 1935. He married Amanda Susan White, a farmer's daughter from Dalwood, on 19 December 1888 at Axminster Register Office; they had 15 children, all baptised at Widworthy Church. The eldest was Frank whose birth certificate shows that he was born on 28 March 1890 at 'Colwell Cottage, Offwell'. The younger children were William Thomas (born 1892), Edwin Frederick (born 1894), Albert James (born 1895), Charles Edgar (born 1897), Florence Anna (born 1898), Maud and Victor George (born 1902), Emily (born 1903), Archibald and Leonard (born 1904), Dorothy Gladys (born 1909), Robert (born 1911), Ernest John and Evelyn Amanda (born 4 April 1913).

Kelly's Directory for the year 1910 lists Thomas Dare as gamekeeper for E H M Luckock, the tenant at Widworthy Court. An article in the *Exeter and Plymouth Gazette* from March 1912 recorded the departure of Mr and Mrs Luckock:

> LOSS TO WIDWORTHY
> The departure of Mr and Mrs Luckock from Widworthy Court to a property in Monmouthshire, lately purchased by Mr Luckock, was felt to be a fitting opportunity for the expression of the sentiments of regard entertained for them by the parishioners of Widworthy. Accordingly, a gathering of parishioners and friends from the neighbourhood was held in the school, and presided over by the Rector, the Rev L Green...[122]

'Mr and Mrs Dare' were listed among those present at this ceremony, at which the Luckocks were presented with a rose bowl inscribed with their crest and an inscription expressing the 'regard and esteem' of the donors.

Thomas Dare later worked for Lady Peek, who leased Widworthy Court in the early 1920s from the Marwood-Elton family. This was the Honourable Augusta Louisa (born 1854), eldest daughter of the 8th Viscount Midleton and widow of Sir Cuthbert Peek (died 1901), 2nd baronet. *Kelly's Directory 1919* lists Thomas Dare as gamekeeper to her second son, Roger Grenville Peek (born 1888), who must have been living with his mother after seeing active service as a captain in the 9th Lancers in the First World War (during which he was taken prisoner). Captain Peek served as Assistant Division Commander to the General Officer Commanding in Chief. He married Joan Penelope Sclater-Booth of Ivybridge, Devon, on 16 January 1919 but was killed only two years later while on duty in Ireland, on 23 March 1921. He left two sons, one of whom (Roger John Peek) was also killed in action, in Libya in 1942. Lady Peek died on 3 November 1934, by which time she had moved to Hembury Fort House, in the parish of Buckerell, near Honiton. She left a personal estate valued at £17,695. In 1935 her daughter Kathleen Marian was living at Hembury Fort House. Hembury

---

[122] *Exeter and Plymouth Gazette*, 22 March 1912, page 12.

Fort, coincidentally, had been the residence of Admiral Samuel Graves (died 1787), great-uncle to Mary Graves; there is a monument to him in parish church at Buckerell.

Mr and Mrs Thomas Dare

After the departure of the Peeks from Widworthy, Thomas Dare worked directly for the Marwood-Elton family; he was listed as gamekeeper to 'Col Elton' (William Marwood-Elton) in *Kelly's Directory 1923* and as gamekeeper to Lt-Col Marwood-Elton in 1926. His home was Knapp Cottage, Widworthy, but while this was being renovated he lived in Colwell Wood Cottage. *Kelly's Directory 1935* lists Thomas and Victor Dare respectively as gamekeeper and woodman to Mrs Marwood-Elton. Thomas Dare died in 1935.

The Dare family of Offwell has been said to have had a genealogical connection with Virginia Dare, born 20 August 1587 at Roanoke in Virginia (now modern North Carolina), and celebrated as the first English child born in North America. For the purposes of this study, a limited investigation of the Dare genealogy has been carried out and the results are set out briefly at Appendix E.

In the 1980s the youngest of the 15 Dare children, Evelyn (born 1913), who married Thomas Alfred Sweetland of Axminster (who was born on 25 February 1888, the son of Henry Sweetland), could recall the shooting parties of her father's day, when the gentlemen were accompanied by butlers to serve their meals. Thomas Dare's duties included training the gun dogs and feeding the pheasants; his children were given the task of boiling, shelling and sieving hens' eggs for the birds' feed. Frank Dare, the eldest child, who was born at the Cottage, married Alice Mary Ann Stamp on 29 July 1913. Alice, who then lived at Seaton, was the daughter of, who was a sawyer; whether she was related to the Stamps of Colwell Wood Cottage is not known.

Later Tenants

The Cottage seems to have seen several different occupants in the late nineteenth century. The 1891 census shows James Curtis, a woodsman, with his family, living there:

Census 5 April 1891
TNA RG 12 1671, fol 94, page 2
Schedule No 10: Colwell Wood Cottage, Offwell (4 rooms occupied)

				Occupation	*Where born*
James Curtis	Head	M	44	Woodsman	Devon, Fremington
Grace Curtis	Wife	M	[?]56[123]		*D[itt]o* Torrington
Gertrude Curtis	Daur	S	26	General Servant (Domestic)	*Do Do*
John Curtis	Son		15		Dorset, St Giles in the Wood
Silas Curtis	Son		13		*Do Do*

The electoral registers show that James Curtis occupied the Cottage between 1890 and 1894. It will be seen from the birth places of his children that the family had been fairly mobile, although St Giles in the Wood is in fact in north Devon, not Dorset. James himself came from Fremington, near Barnstaple in north Devon. Earlier census returns and civil registration indexes show that Grace was his second wife: he had married his first wife, Catherine Sussex, in 1867 and the 1881 census shows them living in the hamlet of Kingscott, St Giles in the Wood.

Catherine Curtis, who was working as a gloveress in 1871, died in 1880 in St Giles in the Wood and James (whose surname was sometimes spelled Curtice) married Grace Ward in the Torrington district of North Devon at the end of 1881; Grace too was a gloveress, and the 1881 census indicates that she had not been previously married, although she had two children. Great Torrington was an important centre of Devon's glove-making industry in the nineteenth century.

James was described as an agricultural labourer in the 1871 census (when they were already in Kingscott), and a labourer in 1881, so he does not appear to have had extensive experience as a woodsman. His son Silas had a twin brother, Paul, but Gertrude Curtis, the servant shown in 1891 as James's daughter, was his step-daughter.

Grace Curtis died a few years after this census was taken: her death was registered in the first quarter of 1895 in the Honiton district and her age was said to be 59. What became of James Curtis after that is not clear, but he appears to have moved on again. The 1911 census shows that his son Silas joined the army and married.

Electoral registers show that the Cottage was occupied by a man called Doswell in 1896/7 and we may guess that he took over James Curtis's job as woodsman.

---

[123] This number has been heavily struck through: it might read '52'. In 1881 Grace was said to have been 42; in 1895, she was said to have been 59.

When the 1901 census was taken, a Skinner family was living in Colwell Wood; Fred Skinner was not a woodsman but a gamekeeper:

Census 31 March 1901
TNA RG 13 2023 fol 14
Schedule No 68: Colwell Wood, Offwell

				Occupation	*Where born*	
Fred Skinner	Head	M	45	Game Keeper	[Devon] Ottery St Mary	
Emma Skinner	Wife	M	47		*Do*	*Do*
Sophia R Skinner	Daur	S	20	Dress maker (worker)	*Do*	Sidbury
Frank Burroughs	Visitor	S	23	Pte, 2nd Devonshire Regiment	*Do*	Shute

The 1891 census shows that Fred had been a gamekeeper in his previous job, in Branscombe, Devon, and he had then been assisted in his work by his 15-year-old son and namesake. The electoral registers confirm that Fred Skinner lived at the Cottage between 1901 and 1902, after which date William White moved in, remaining there until 1905. The 1911 census shows that Emma Skinner had died and Fred was now a gamekeeper in the parish of Yarcombe, Devon.

The electoral registers make no mention of the Cottage or Colwell Wood for the years 1906 or 1907, so it may have been empty during these years. In 1908 Thomas Sparkes is listed at a dwelling house in Colwell Wood; this is his only appearance in the records.

It has been estimated that at this period (1905), just under 90,000 acres of Devon was still woodland. Despite the devastations of two wars and the disintegration of many large estates, in the period 1947–49 the area of private woodland still amounted to nearly 92,000 acres.[124]

It is not quite clear who (if anyone) was living in Colwell Wood Cottage at the time of the 1911 census; there appears to be no household listed with this address. However, the electoral registers for the period 1905 to 1915 show that a James Richards lived at 'Colwell Cottage'. This probably refers to a cottage close to the site of the mill beside Offwell Brook, since in 1915 James Richards's address was 'Colwell Cottage & Mill Cottage'. The census of 1911 shows James, a general labourer, living at 'Colwell Cottage, Offwell', with his wife Ellen, son Luke and two grandchildren. There is nothing in the census schedule to help determine the exact location of 'Colwell Cottage'.

The Inland Revenue 'Domesday'

At about this time, an assessment of Colwell Wood Cottage was undertaken as part of the massive Inland Revenue Valuation Office survey, initiated by Lloyd George's Finance (1909–1910) Act. This was a national survey for tax purposes[125] which recorded all property in the United Kingdom

---

[124] W G Hoskins, *Devon* (1954, revised 2003), page 304.

[125] The main object of the Act was to tax the capital appreciation of real property (increment value duty). The valuation excluded any appreciation attributable to crops, buildings and improvements paid for by the owners. Increment value duty was fiercely resisted by landowners and repealed by the 1920 Finance Act. Thus the original assessment was annotated with notes from later inspections.

and became known as the 'new Domesday'. The main object was to tax the capital appreciation of real property (increment value duty). The valuation excluded any appreciation attributable to crops, buildings and improvements paid for by the owners.

Landowners were initially sent a form, which had to be completed or a penalty of £50 was charged. The information they provided was to be used as a baseline for assessing later increases in value. The owner's information was copied into a field book and an inspection was subsequently made – in this case in May 1912 – to check the details and add further notes.

The following entry is from the valuer's field book, with the inspector's annotations from 1912 shown in italics:[126]

Colwell Wood Cottage

Description:	Cottage, garden and pheasantry
Extent:	2 acres 2 roods 14 perches *2a 2r 13p*
Rateable value, buildings:	£11 2s 6d
Occupier:	E H M Luckock *Not occupied dec'd*
Owner:	Rev A Marwood Elton
	now Maj Wm Marwood Elton, Heathfield, Taunton
Interest of owner:	F [freehold] Life
Actual [or estimated] rent:	'Included in lease for Widworthy Court and included in return for Widworthy parish'
Outgoings:	Land Tax: not known
Tithe:	2s 1d paid by owner

Rates & taxes are paid by tenant; insurance is paid by owner; repairs are paid for jointly

Particulars, description and notes made on inspection, May 1912
P[art] Widworthy Court

Cottage & garden, OS[127] 161:	.263a
Pheasantry, OS 161:	.956a
— [blank], OS 163:	1.368a
Total:	2.587a

'Keeper's cottage now vacant, stone built & thatched, 2 down & up, with boiling house and linhay[128] adj[oining] wood & tiled. In moderate repair. EC or outhouse detached near, wood & tiled, poor; and 2 stall stable below wood or galviron, fair. Pheasantry of wire netting divided into 10 runs'

Charges, easements and restrictions affecting market value of fee simple:
'now in a dilapidated state'. Tithe: 2s 1d x 20 yp = say £2'

Valuation: Market value of fee simple in possession of whole property in its present condition: 'say £100'
Deduct market value of site: £20
Proportion of market value attributable to structures, timber etc: £20
Buildings and structures worth: £80

---

[126] Offwell Assessment, The National Archives IR 58/30470, Ref 61.

[127] OS: Ordnance Survey (Field Number).

[128] Linhay: an open-fronted outbuilding or shed.

Market value of fee simple of whole in its present condition: £100
Additional value: charges: Tithe: £2
Gross value: £102

It seems clear from this that the Cottage was uninhabited, but not altogether dilapidated, in May 1912. E H M Luckock, shown as the original occupier, was the tenant of Widworthy Court and apparently died before May 1912.

The Inland Revenue field books mention the pheasantry, which covered the small one-acre field just to the south-east of the Cottage and its small garden; this was divided into ten runs. We do not know precisely when the pheasantry was established; it was not labelled as such on the first edition of the Ordnance Survey six-inch map (surveyed in 1888 and published in 1889) but on the second edition (revised in 1903 and published in 1906) it is placed in the woods, to the east of the lower of the two fields to the south-east of the Cottage.

The Pheasantry after modern restoration

The 1891 census described James Curtis who lived at Colwell Wood Cottage as a woodsman, whereas ten years later, when the 1901 census was taken, the occupant of the Cottage, Fred Skinner, was a gamekeeper; their different occupations probably reflect the introduction of pheasants. The 1906 map also shows 'Kennels' just to the north of the Cottage's small garden.

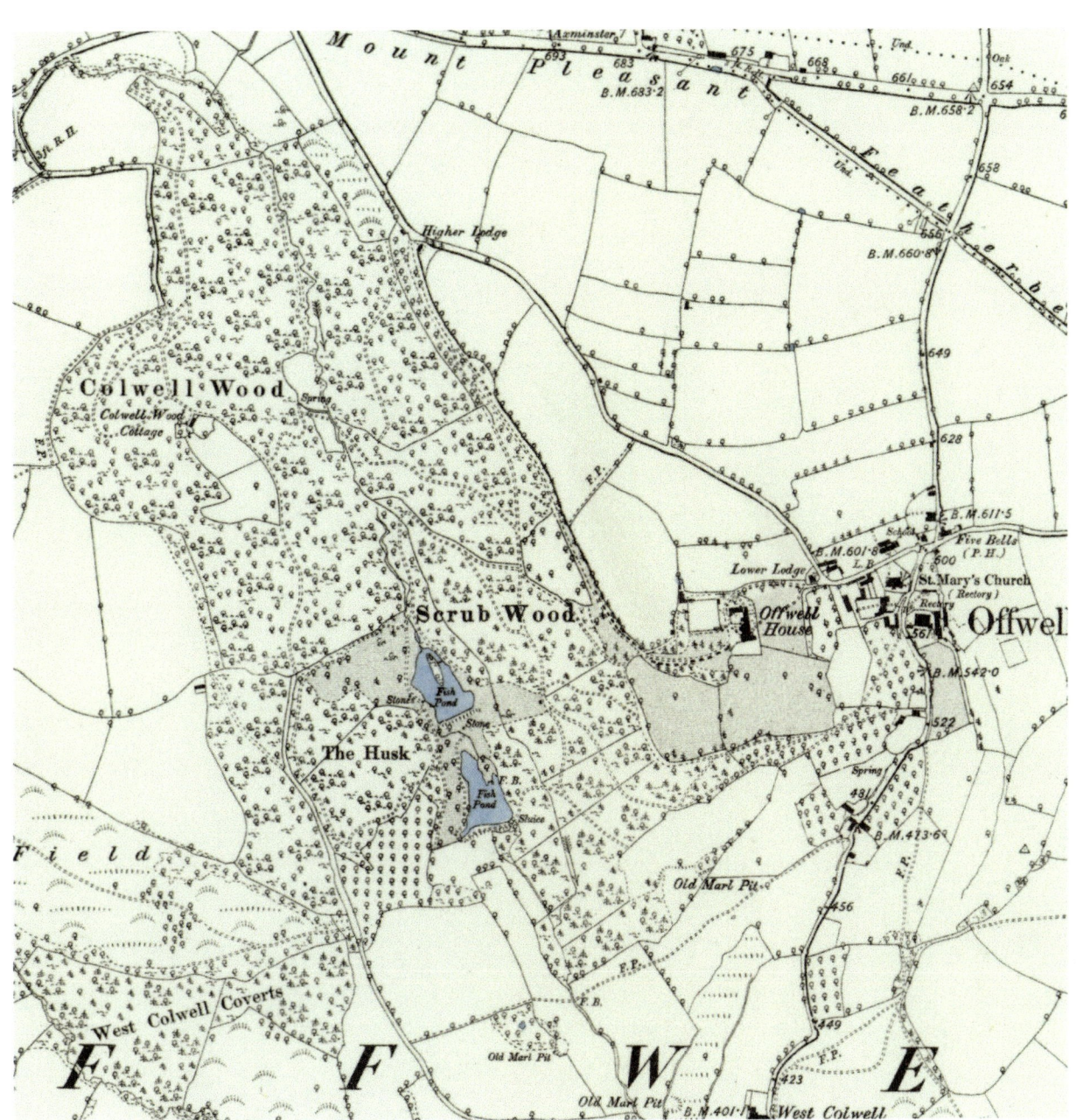

Colwell Wood: 6 inch Ordnance Survey 1889 (surveyed 1888)[129]

[129] Devonshire LXXI.NW. Reproduced by permission of the National Library of Scotland.

83

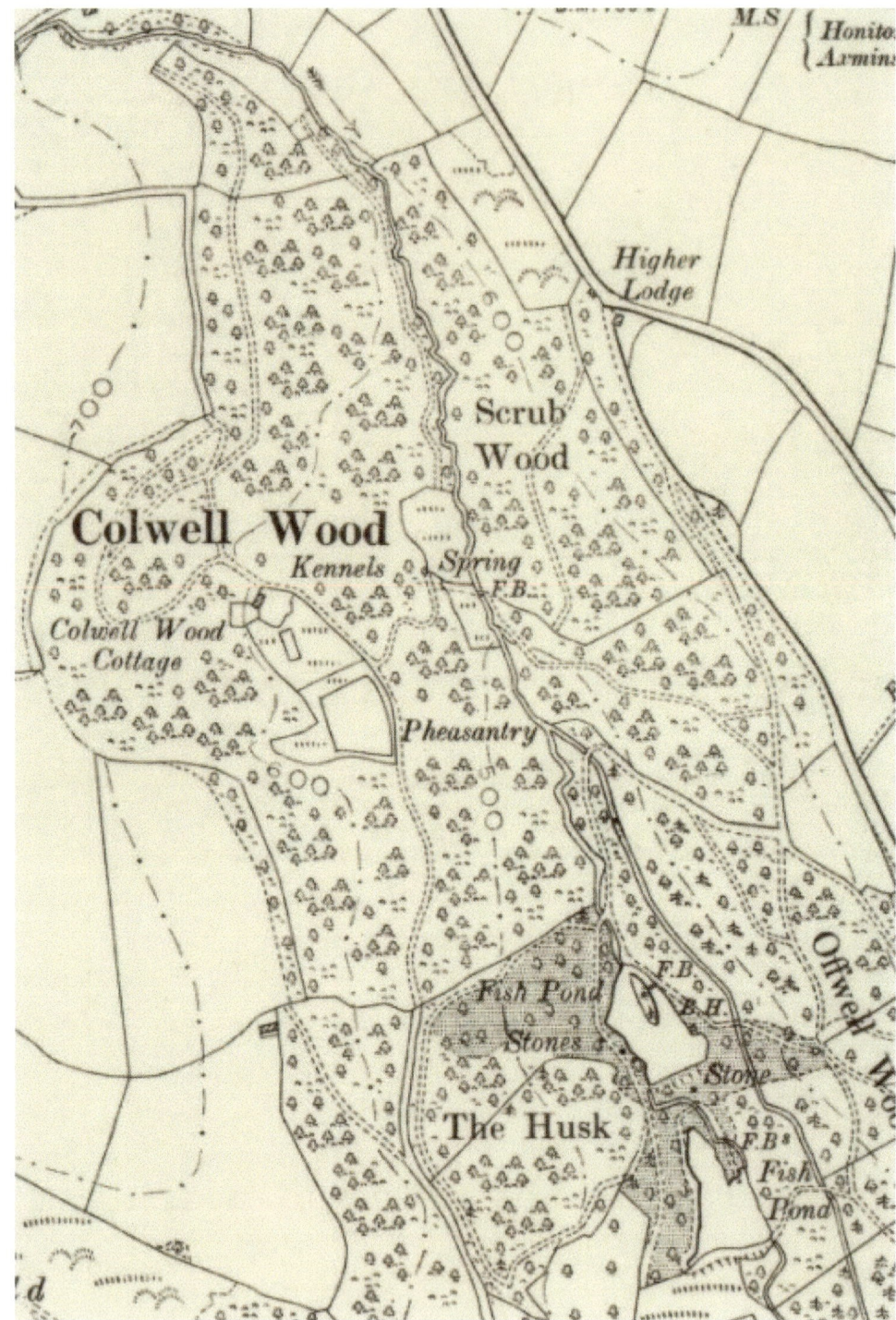

Colwell Wood: 6 inch Ordnance Survey 1906 (surveyed 1903) [130]

---

[130] Devonshire LXXI.NW. Reproduced by permission of the National Library of Scotland.

THE
MARWOOD≈ELTON FAMILY

From 'BURKE'S LANDED GENTRY (1952)
Owners of Colwell Wood are underlined

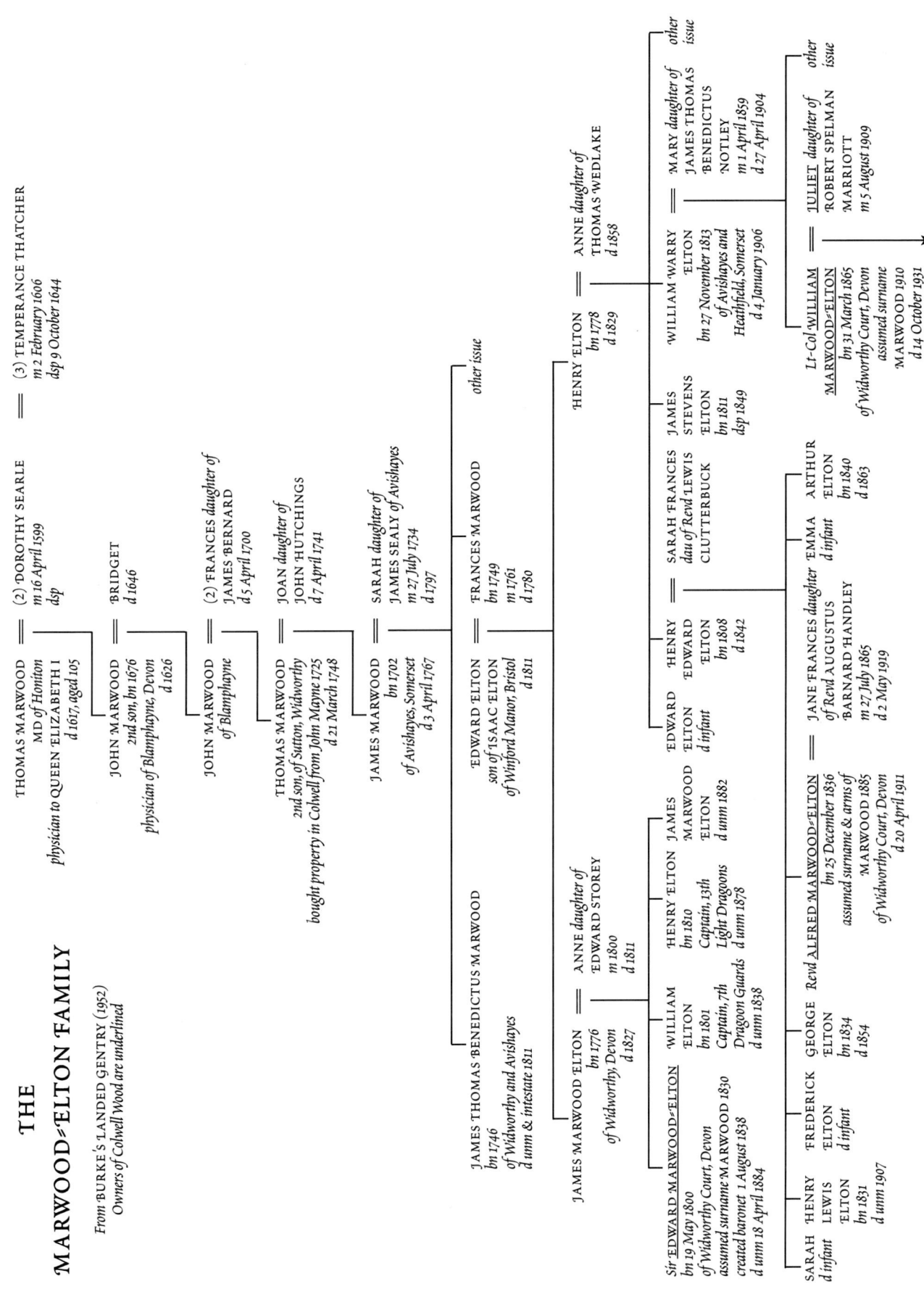

CHAPTER FIVE: THE MARWOOD-ELTON ERA

Early Twentieth Century Ownership

To return to the Marwood-Elton family, after the death of the Revd Alfred Marwood-Elton in April 1911 the Widworthy estate passed to his first cousin Lieutenant-Colonel William (Marwood) Elton, son of William Warry Elton who had died in 1906. In anticipation of this inheritance, while both William Warry Elton and Alfred Marwood-Elton were still living, a disentailing deed had been enacted on 20 May 1904 whereby the estate was placed into the hands of a trustee for the use of William Elton.

As part of this agreement, William Elton:

> absolutely renounced and abandoned his surname of Elton and declared that he had assumed and adopted and intended thenceforth on all occasions whatsoever to use and subscribe the name of Marwood-Elton instead of Elton.

A deed poll effecting this change was however not enrolled until 18 June 1910.

In the meantime, another sale had taken place: on 29 September 1906, William Dommett of Weston-super-Mare had sold to Major William Elton fourteen acres of 'scrubwood' in Offwell. These comprised two plots (153 and 154 on the Ordnance Survey, 246 and 286 on the Tithe Map): the first was described as furze (2a 1r 30p) and the second as wood (11a 3r). The selling price was £200. These lands, known as Scrub Wood, became part of the Widworthy estate and are now part of the present Colwell Wood Cottage estate.

William Elton, later Marwood-Elton, was born on 31 March 1865, the son of William Warry Elton (1813–1906) and his wife Mary, daughter of James Thomas Benedictus Notley. After an education at Sherborne School and Trinity Hall, Cambridge, he joined The Welch (Welsh) Regiment and served in the Anglo-Boer Wars (1899–1902) and in the First World War. At the time of the disentailing deed (1904) he was a major of the 3rd Battalion, Welsh Regiment, of Heathfield, near Taunton. This refers to the family home of Heathfield (Lodge) in the village of Hillfarance, near Taunton; William was living there with his elderly parents at the time of the 1891 census.

On 9 August 1909 William married Juliet, daughter of Robert Spelman Marriott, and the 1911 census shows them at Heathfield, a house of 18 rooms, with their eldest child, Beryl, and three servants, as well as Juliet's aunt. The Inland Revenue field book (see above, page 81) shows Major William Marwood Elton living in 'Heathfield, Taunton', but the family later took up residence at Widworthy Court.

After the First World War, many large country estates were broken up. A substantial part of the Widworthy Court estate, comprising 18 farms and smallholdings amounting to 2,650 acres, was sold on 21 May 1919, but Colwell Wood was not part of the estate sold at this time.

Colonel William Marwood-Elton died on 14 October 1931 at the age of 66. His funeral reflected both his military honours and his love of the local countryside: he was buried in a coffin of unpolished English oak, on which was placed the Union Jack, his helmet, medals and sword. His hearse was a farm wagon drawn by two horses and the village schoolchildren lined the pathway to Widworthy church.[131]

The Colonel had recently made a will (dated 5 August 1931 and proved 15 February 1932) by which his widow, Mrs Juliet Marwood-Elton, inherited a life interest in the Widworthy Court estate. Included in this were Colwell Wood Cottage and lands (3.591 acres) and Offwell Woods. The latter formed part of an extensive woodland estate, comprising land in Offwell, Dalwood, Colyton and Shute, described as plantations and woods with a total of just over 266 acres. Mrs Marwood-Elton continued to live at Widworthy Court with her son, Nigel William David Marwood-Elton (born 22 August 1911).

The Tuke Family

From 1920 Samuel Tuke, whose address was given as the Devon and Exeter Club, Exeter, was listed as of Colwell Wood in the electoral registers. In 1921 and 1922 an additional entry gives the name of his wife, Violet May Tuke, as of the same address. These entries refer to Colwell House, built by Samuel Tuke in 1920 adjacent to the Wood; he had previously lived at Netherton Hall, Farway.

The Tuke family, whose pedigree is set out in *Burke's Landed Gentry* (1937) descends from Robert Tuke of Scotton, Yorkshire, who died in 1605. Samuel, who later became a Justice of the Peace, was born on 6 August 1854, the son of James Hack Tuke and his wife, Elizabeth, formerly Janson. Samuel was educated at Trinity College, Cambridge, and married Violet, elder daughter of Captain E W D Croke of Ballynagarde, County Limerick, Ireland, in 1897. They had three children, these being Bryan James Edward Danzil Tuke (born 1900), Francis Samuel Galfrid Tuke who was a lieutenant in the Royal Navy (born 1901) and Edward Christopher William Tuke (born 1903).

Samuel Tuke died in November 1937 at Colwell House. His obituary in the *Exeter and Plymouth Gazette* describes him as 'of a kindly disposition' and noted that he supported many local organisations and the charitable institutions of the neighbourhood. All three of his sons married and had issue. Edward's son Lt-Cdr Barry Tuke now lives at Colwell House.

Jack Hawkins

Meanwhile Colwell Wood Cottage was occupied by John Hawkins, known as Jack, who was a smallholder, and might at one time have been an employee of the Marwood-Eltons. His tenure was a long one, from 1923 to 1938, according to the electoral registers. Local sources recall that he kept a pony and raised chickens at the Cottage; that he also ploughed up some of the surrounding land, possibly claiming a little more than he should have done, by ring-barking the odd tree; and that he sold vegetables.

---

[131] *Exeter and Plymouth Gazette*, 17 October 1931.

Towards the end of his life, Hawkins succumbed to alcoholism. The *Western Times* of 8 October 1937 reported that he had been found lying in the middle of the road in Honiton:

> John Hawkins, a 66-years-old labourer, of Offwell's Wood [*sic*], was summoned at the local sessions Wednesday for being drunk and incapable. Supt Willcocks said defendant had had eight previous convictions for drunkenness, and when he was released on bail he went immediately to a public house. A little later witness saw him staggering up New-street, hardly able to get along.

The magistrates bound the defendant over for twelve months, a condition being that he must not enter a public house. He was also ordered to pay 10d costs.

Less than a year later, Jack Hawkins appeared at much greater length in the *Exeter and Plymouth Gazette* under the heading:

> Allegations That Man Was "Set Alight." Denials at Adjourned Hearing: No Drunken Spree or Skylarking.

Sadly, John Hawkins had died, after an incident in a cellar at Hawley Farm in nearby Dalwood, where he was accustomed to visit regularly. He had gone to the farm door, on a September Sunday morning, to ask for a drink of cider from Walter John Clapp. He had a drink (the cider was laced with parsnip wine) and some bread and cheese but returned later in the afternoon with three other men (Ted Langford, Frank Reed and Hugo Reed, who was eighteen) in a car. The four men were smoking in the cellar when Hawkins was said to have sworn and threatened one of the other men, Ted Langford, with a knife, and then fell, upsetting some oil which poured over him. He was smoking a pipe and his shirt somehow – the inquest was unable to determine exactly how – began to smoulder. The other men's accounts of the incident were vague and contradictory. Hawkins did not die in the cellar but appeared again at the farm the next morning seeking his pipe, which had broken when he fell. He said that he had not been home and that he felt 'rough, shivery and cold'. He was admitted to Honiton Infirmary on 7 September and died just over a week later, on 15 September 1938. The cause of death was 'hypostatic pneumonia accelerated by burns'. Jack Hawkins was said at the inquest to have lived 'in a very rough manner, like a wild man, in a hut in the woods at Offwell, and obtained a shilling or two by keeping poultry'. When the foreman at the inquest asked a witness whether Hawkins was 'mentally affected', he replied 'a little, I should say'.

Jack Hawkins was buried in an unmarked grave in Offwell churchyard on 18 September 1938; the register described him as aged 67 and of Colwell Wood Cottage.

The *Exeter and Plymouth Gazette* of 31 January 1936 printed a reminder of how the more privileged local inhabitants were passing their time, with an account of a fox-hunt in which the hounds:

> raced away after one [fox] across the road into Offwell Woods, back to the road again into Lomans Brake, near the course of the Honiton Golf Club, back to Poltimore Gorse, down through the valley, right-handed across the valley of Appledore, by the side of the hill to Lomans Brake, on to Colwell and Offwell Woods, near Offwell House and Offwell Church, to the top end of the stone quarry, and Sutton Farm. From the top of an ivy-covered stump over-hanging

a pond, the fox, surrounded by hounds, jumped into the water and was killed after a run of two hours and fifty minutes. It was a slow but interesting hunt, hounds picking up the line and working it out prettily. Mrs Broom, wife of a former Master of the Hunt, was presented with the mask.

Sale of Colwell Wood to George Blay Ltd

While Jack Hawkins had been sliding towards the sad and muddled end to his life, the history of Colwell Wood Cottage had also been approaching the end of an era and the 'hut in the woods' that had been his home for many years had been sold. On 6 July 1937 Colwell Wood and Scrub Wood were offered for sale by the Marwood-Elton family. They formed 'Lot 22' in the auction of 'The Outlying Portions of the Widworthy estate', comprising about 1,350 acres in all, and they were described as:

> A Valuable Area of Woodland known as Colwell Wood situate in the Parish of Offwell with an approach from the Offwell Road. The Wood contains a quantity of matured timber and young plantations of oak, beech etc. The whole extends to an area of approximately 69 acres.[132]

This included the two plots of 'scrubwood' that had been sold by William Dommett to Major William Elton in 1906, and this conveyance was noted in the sale particulars. The auction took place at the Dolphin Hotel in Honiton.

In the Deed of Conveyance, which was dated 29 October 1937, the Cottage was described as merely a 'building', and a pheasantry and spring were mentioned together with the 'woodland' in Colwell Wood and Scrub Wood. The sale was reported in the *Exeter and Plymouth Gazette*:

> PORTIONS OF WIDWORTHY SOLD
> Spirited Biddings for Farms and Land
>
> Considerable interest was aroused in the sale at the Dolphin Hotel, Honiton, on Tuesday, of the outlying portions of the Widworthy estate, extending to an area of 1,350 acres.
> ... The auctioneer said it had been called by the direction of Mrs Marwood Elton. He thought the name of Widworthy and Marwood Elton had been synonymous since 1506. They regretted the splitting up of these estates, but they had held on to the Widworthy estate considerably longer than others...
> .... Colwell Wood, Offwell, 69 acres, and a cottage, to Mr W E Brown, for £2,250.
> The solicitors concerned were Messrs Tweed and Son, Honiton.[133]

Mr W E Brown was probably an agent, for at this date the property passed into the ownership of George Blay Limited, a sawmill company based in Honiton which had only recently become incorporated. George Blay, who traded under his own name or as Messrs George Blay, had died just a year before the sale.

---

[132] Devon Archives 547B/p/3828/i: see partial copy at Appendix F.
[133] *Exeter and Plymouth Gazette*, 9 July 1937, page 14.

George Blay was an enterprising timber merchant who was born in Reading in 1880, the son of Thomas and Louisa Blay. He had begun his career as a commercial traveller for a timber merchant and dealt successfully in government surplus. The *Western Morning News* on 25 August 1922 carried a notice advertising:

> Surplus Government stocks of bow huts, black corrugated iron, steel shelters, &c., are being offered at bargain prices by Messrs George Blay, Honiton.

Prior to the First World War, with the building industry generally in decline, Blay had established a business at New Malden, Surrey, constructing timber buildings. After the war he recognised the potential of the coming housing boom ahead of many other builders, and his company, Cannon Hill Estates Ltd, worked on an audaciously large scale to develop the London suburb of Raynes Park, built on the site of the Raynes Park Golf Club (which he purchased in 1924) and a number of adjacent areas. Here he aimed to build between 150 and 200 houses a year, a scale which enabled him to obtain favourable mortgage rates for his buyers. [134]

George Blay had started his sawmill company in Honiton, which later became George Blay Ltd, on the site of a scrap yard, with the aim of providing local employment. The local newspapers of 1918 show him advertising for sawyers, for a portable steam engine, for timber carriages and horses, and in the same columns Mrs (Olive) Blay of The Link House, Raynes Park, was seeking a cook-general (£36) and a house parlour-maid (£30).

The initial investment of £500 was given to John Robert Maeer, the first Managing Director, on the understanding that if the money ran out, more would be invested. John Robert Maeer was also chairman of the Federated Home Timber Association. A steam generator – the first in Honiton – was bought at Earls Court, London, to power the mill.

George Blay died at The Manor House in Ditton Hill, Surrey, on 25 July 1936, at the age of 56, leaving a personal estate worth nearly £400,000.

After George Blay's death, Mr Maeer continued to steer the company through difficult times and good ones. During the Second World War the company was advertising for haulage and for timber as well as the sale of small timber outbuildings:

> POULTRY AND PIG HOUSES. Garden huts and any Building connected with the war effort. Catalogue free. George Blay Ltd, Desk 5, Honiton. [135]

> STANDING TIMBER, Oak, Ash and Beech, preferably Plantation. State size and quantity for cash – George Blay Ltd, Honiton 2393. [136]

---

[134] J R Tarling, 'Building Raynes Park', Raynes Park and West Barnes Residents' Association website. This article is incorrect in stating that Blay was born in Devon.
[135] *Western Morning News*, 7 January 1942, page 4.
[136] *Western Times*, 2 May 1941.

> PRICE required for haultage of 3,000 tons of small Fir Poles, Tree Lengths, from Posbury to Crediton Station. Weekly cheques – Further particulars from George Blay Ltd, Honiton.[137]

By 1941, when the saw mills were saved from a serious fire, the firm had 60 employees.

The company extracted large quantities of timber from Colwell Wood during the Second World War, and also during the years 1959 to 1960.

The company continued to buy local woodland and the *Western Times* on 3 February 1950 reported the discovery of:

> A rare tree on the Widworthy estate, recently purchased by George Blay Ltd, electric saw mills, Honiton... the Royal Botanical Gardens identifies it as a species of hickory, namely shagbark hickory... the species from which axle spokes are made... At least two of the collectors applied to Mr Maeer for small pieces to add to their collection.

In 1970 Maeer was succeeded by his son, John Raymond Maeer, who had worked for the company (with a break for war service) since 1939.

As manufacturers of wood products, George Blay Ltd continued to trade into the present century and was finally dissolved in 2012.

---

[137] *Express and Echo*, 16 September 1940.

Chapter Six
RECENT HISTORY

Twentieth Century Tenants

During and after the Second World War, the occupants of the Cottage were William Henry Chick, who had retired in 1937, and his wife Lily; they succeeded the unfortunate Jack Hawkins as tenants. The Chicks had seven children: Beatrice, William junior (Bill) who set off from the Cottage to join the Army in 1939, Lilly, Arnold, Albert, Frances and Lionel.   The Offwell burial register shows that William Henry Chick of Colwell Cottage was buried on 18 September 1945 aged 68.

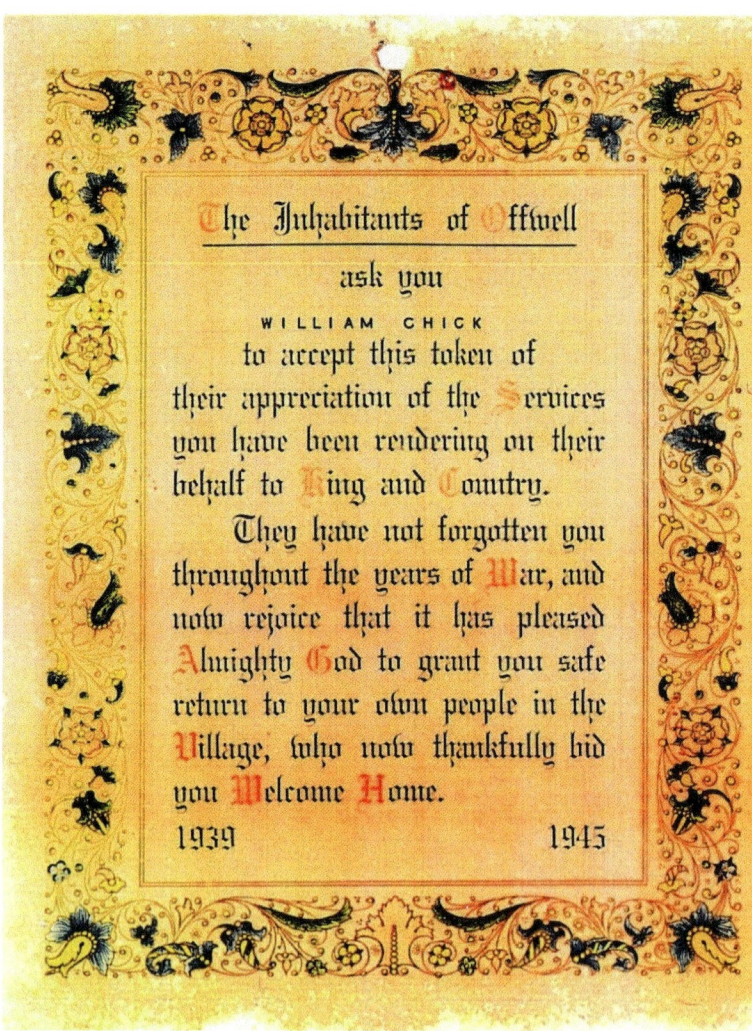

Offwell's vote of thanks to William Chick

The Chick family have preserved a decorated vote of thanks from 'The Inhabitants of Offwell' to William Chick to welcome him on his safe return from the war. In peacetime William worked as a driver for Whiteways Cider; he retired in 1987.

William's brother Arnold Chick (1924–1982) served in the Home Guard during the war.[138]

When William Blay senior died, his sons, Bill, Albert and Lionel, helped to shoulder his coffin through the woods to Offwell church.

The successors to the Chicks at the Cottage were the Brices: in 1951 the electoral register shows Cyril and Beatrice Brice living in 'The Cottage, Offwell Woods', which probably refers to Colwell Wood. Neighbours in the 1980s recalled that Mr Brice kept poultry and had a shed and garage at the fork of the cottage track.

---

[138] Belinda Bennett, 'Legend: Arnold Chick', *Midweek Herald*, 6 February 2013.

Local sources state that from 1953 to 1955 a Mr Reedman, who was employed by George Blay Limited, lived in the Cottage, which was flooded in 1954. His daughter Barbara (who in 1966 became Mrs Barbara M Hawker) lived there as a young child. However, the electoral registers for the years 1952 to 1954 show no-one at Colwell Wood or Colwell Wood Cottage.

Fom 1955 to 1958, John Henning was listed in the electoral registers as the occupier of the Cottage, and in 1955 Frideswide Henning, who was perhaps his wife or daughter, was also registered as a voter there.

From 1959 to 1965 the electoral registers show that the occupants of the Cottage were Harry and Winifred Whitham (née Silvers), who came from Sheffield. Harry (born 1898) was a glass cutter at the Devon Lady glass factory in Talewater. Listed with the Whithams in 1961 was Nellie Silvers, Winifred's elderly mother, who died in 1961 at the age of 81.

Arnold, son of William Henry and Lily Chick, returned with a companion to live at the Cottage in about 1967[139] and remained there until his death in 1982,[140] paying £1 a week in rent. Arnold Ernest J Chick, who was born on 1 May 1924, worked as a timber mate for George Blay Limited and is still recalled affectionately as a harmless but dishevelled figure, in a flat cap and overcoat tied with string, who played the accordion and harmonica, and was frequently the worse for wear after visiting the Honiton pubs.[141] He cycled daily from Colwell Wood to Honiton, where he was employed as a skilled log packer at the George Blay Ltd sawmills.

After Arnold Chick's death, the Cottage stood empty for several years and became derelict.

Sale and Restoration

In 1978 George Blay Ltd acquired a portion of Offwell Woods, bordering Offwell House and parallel to Ramsden Lane, from the Wiggan Trustees, these being Charles Michael Wiggan of Downham House, Downham, and Hugh de Vere Welchman.

Finally, W L Hutton acquired Colwell Wood Cottage, Colwell Wood, Scrub Wood and the narrow eastern portion of Offwell Woods, all of which amounted to approximately 75 acres, on 7 June 1985, at which point the Cottage was unoccupied and had no mains electricity, water or gas. The price paid was £80,000.

In 1985, the thatched roof of the Cottage was covered by corrugated iron. The walls are rendered flint and there were oak beams in the roof, and oak door posts and a lintel. There was also a wooden shed with a loft and a red-tiled roof. As many as possible of the original fabric of the building and its fittings were preserved during the restoration process. Original floor tiles were reused to tile the hearth and front porch.

---

[139] Or possibly from January 1971.
[140] From the General Register Office Indexes to deaths, December quarter, 1982: Exeter 21 1141.
[141] Belinda Bennett, 'Legend: Arnold Chick', *Midweek Herald*, 6 February 2013.

Above (front) and below (back): Colwell Wood Cottage before its restoration in 1985

An oak beam which supports the upper floor shows uneven chamfering, indicating that like many old timbers it had once served some other purpose. There is an elm beam over the fireplace which bears the name 'John Sanford'. This name has not emerged among the known occupiers or owners of the Cottage, but Sanford is certainly a Devon surname.[142] One end of the beam is supported by Beer stone; on the other are two iron chimney bars on which cooking pots once hung.

The hearth and bread oven in Colwell Wood Cottage

A bread oven has been preserved, with an iron door which bears the name 'Huxtable and Sons, Honiton and Fairmile'. This firm probably originated with William Huxtable, who appears in the 1851 census of Fair Mile, Talaton, as a machine maker: among his household were two carpenters and a smith who were described as his servants.[143] The village of Talaton is about eleven miles north-east of Exeter. By 1881 this same William Huxtable was described in the census as an agricultural implement maker, and the *Western Times* for 22 May 1878 included the following advertisement for their stand at the Devon County Agricultural Show:

> William Huxtable & Sons, Fair Mile Implement Works & Iron Foundry, Honiton
> Beg to inform their Friends that they will Exhibit at the above Stands a Specimen Collection Implements and Machines, calculated for the Western Counties...

---

[142] The 1911 census shows an entry which might be significant: a John Sanford, widower, born in Exeter in about 1860/1, was working as timber merchant's carter and living in St Thomas, Exeter. The National Archives RG 14 12650 Schedule Number 117.
[143] The National Archives HO 107 1864 fol 63 page 10.

An oak chest was made, by Mr Alan Poulton, from some of the roof trusses and door post timbers that could not be preserved in their original function. Among the oddments found during the restoration work was a Mappin and Webb silver pepper pot, hallmarked 'Birmingham 1926'. In 1986, electricity, well water and telephone services were brought to the Cottage. By 1987 it was restored and used for guests.

Above: Owner and friends at Colwell Wood Cottage in 1986; Below: the Cottage after restoration

Colwell Wood Cottage today

In April 1997 the tranquillity and seclusion of Colwell Wood was threatened by an application by Mr Eric Mawer (on behalf of the Ramblers' Association) to Devon County Council to upgrade the existing Public Bridleway No 17 which passes through Colwell Wood to the status of a byway, which would be open to all vehicular traffic, such as motor-bikes and off-road four-wheeled vehicles. This application was robustly opposed by the owner of Colwell Wood, Offwell Parish Council and many other individuals who valued the beauty and peace of the woods, particularly when the bluebells were in flower. The dispute resulted in a good deal of local publicity, such as the front-page headline in *Express and Echo (Honiton Edition)* of Thursday 22 May 1997: 'Village Fury at Ramblers'.

Entrance to Colwell Wood

The bridleway runs from the north-west corner of Colwell Wood, southwards to Colwell Wood Cottage. In 1991 a minor diversion of the old route was permitted; the bridleway was re-directed to the north and east of the small pond behind the Cottage so as to give more privacy to the Cottage. It then joins the old route, which follows the eastern edge of the two small fields to the south-east of the Cottage, and then into the southern portion of Colwell Wood, and eventually to West Colwell. Mr Mawer's application was based on slender documentary evidence from maps and a brief entry in the Offwell Vestry Minute Book of 24 March 1885. Nevertheless, it required a good deal of effort and cost, including the employment of a 'Rights of Way Consultant', to rebut Mr Mawer's application.

The opposition was two-pronged. First, a careful analysis of the maps and documentary sources showed no evidence that the bridleway had ever been a public highway, carriageway or byway, and it had never been maintained as such. Indeed, the gradients and nature of the terrain would never have allowed wheeled traffic to use it regularly, nor could two carts have passed each other.

The second line of defence was a series of witness statements from previous occupiers of the Cottage or those with a personal knowledge of the Cottage and woods going back several decades. William Alfred George Chick, who was born in 1921, lived in Colwell Wood Cottage in the 1930s when his parents were tenants of George Blay Ltd; there was no water or electricity supply to the Cottage at this period. He stated that bridleway was so steep and narrow that even the undertaker, when his father William Henry Chick died in 1945, came on foot to the Cottage and carried the coffin back through the woods to the top of the bridleway. Similarly, the doctor would walk through the woods to reach the Cottage. Mrs Evelyn Sweetland, who was born in 1913, the daughter of Thomas Dare (see Chapter 5) remembered that in places the bridleway was too narrow, rough and steep for vehicles. As the gamekeeper, her father would not allow visitors into the wood for fear of disturbing the pheasants. Several other knowledgeable local people gave written evidence that the bridleway had never carried any vehicular traffic. Mr Mawer's application to upgrade the bridleway to a byway was rejected.

Track to the Pheasantry

This application was part of the Definitive Map Review of public rights of way in Devon, and it was not the only change sought by Mr Mawer of the Ramblers' Association; at the same time, he applied to establish and register several public footpaths in different places in the parish of Offwell. One of these was for a proposed footpath running from the bridleway through Colwell Wood, starting at the eastern edge of the lower of the two small fields to the south of Colwell Wood Cottage, through the woods in a westerly direction to join Ramsden Lane, which is the road to the village of Offwell, at Hillside. The claim was based mainly upon a Diversion Order made by magistrates on 31 May 1826, in respect of a footpath from Colwell Wood to the road. The diversion itself was a very minor one; the footpath has long since disappeared, and its exact route is uncertain. This application was also rejected by Devon County Council for lack of substantial evidence.

The Pond at Colwell Wood Cottage

CONCLUSION

We have traced the history of Colwell, in the parish of Offwell, through nine and a half centuries since it was first mentioned in the Domesday Book. For such a small and often ill-defined place, its history is a rich and varied one, illustrating how research into even the smallest and seemingly most insignificant place in England can reveal a detailed historical narrative.

Strictly speaking, Colwell was never a manor, and since there is no central cluster of houses it is not really a hamlet either; it can loosely be defined as a small estate. Its population, scattered in small farm-houses, cottages and two mills, has probably never exceeded a few dozen people. Throughout its history, its wooded valleys have been a predominant feature in its landscape, and the timber they produced has been an important element in its economy.

During the Middle Ages Colwell was a small fragment within much larger estates owned by great aristocratic families, such as Fitzbaldwin, de Courtenay, Hungerford and Hastings. During the Wars of the Roses, and the period of Yorkist rule between 1461 and 1485, it was held by the ill-fated Richard, Duke of Gloucester, who finally became King Richard III (killed 1485). For these great landowners, Colwell and its woods were probably no more than a name on their steward's schedule, or a receipt on a rent-roll. At the local level, during the thirteenth and fourteenth centuries, we find farmers here with the surnames de Colwell and de Park; they were followed in the fifteenth century by the Dennyng family.

From the sixteenth century onwards, the great aristocratic families were succeeded as landowners in Colwell by several local gentry families, such as Franklin, Collins, Southcott, Marwood and Mayne, each of whom owned portions or fragments of the ancient 'manor' of Colwell. The picture was often a complicated one, with different pieces of the jigsaw changing hands fairly frequently. It was not until 1793/4 that we find evidence of an owner taking a personal interest in Colwell Wood when Admiral Thomas Graves (died 1814) purchased it for £1,210. This was a very high price, which no doubt reflected the valuable timber in the woods. A few years later the Admiral won national fame when, as Lord Nelson's second in command, he achieved a great naval victory at the Battle of Copenhagen on 2 April 1801; *The Times* saluted him as 'a very gallant fellow'.

The appeal of Colwell Wood was twofold. First, its 'fine oak trees' and ancient timber represented a good investment for the future, particularly in an area close to the shipyards in Lyme Regis, Sidmouth and Topsham. Secondly, there was a new element in Colwell's appeal: it was appreciated as a romantic and picturesque rural retreat, and part of its attraction was perhaps that the Admiral found he could gain a distant glimpse of the sea from Colwell Wood. Admiral Graves had just one daughter, Mary (who died in 1860); he gave her the wood in 1805, and it was probably at about this date (and certainly before 1806) that the Graves family built a cottage in Colwell Wood, either as a rural retreat or as a home for their woodman. The steep green wooded dells of Offwell and Colwell were also greatly loved by their neighbour, Edward Copleston, Bishop of Llandaff (died 1849); he has left eloquent testimony to their beauty.

From the early nineteenth century onwards we can trace in some detail the dual functions of Colwell Wood. First it was a practical and valuable asset in its timber and wooded cover for breeding pheasants and game birds, and secondly it was an unspoilt picturesque woodland with its ancient bluebells beneath the canopy of oaks and other trees. By the late twentieth century this second aspect was dominant, and in 1985 Colwell Wood was fortunate in being acquired by an owner who appreciates the natural beauty of the place over and above any commercial interests. He has restored the Cottage, and has striven to preserve its tranquillity and natural habitat for the benefit of future generations.

Nocturnal view from Colwell Wood Cottage

Appendix A

CHRONOLOGICAL TABLES

Table A: Ownership of Colwell to 1657

Date	Tenant in chief	Subtenants
pre 1066	Aelmer	
1086	Baldwin (d 1090)	Rogo
1090	William FitzBaldwin	
–1137	Richard FitzBaldwin (d 1137)	
1242/3	John de Courtenay (d 1274) inherits from father Robert	William de Colwell, followed by Philip de Colwell & Ralph de Colwell
1284–86	Hugh de Courtenay (d 1291)	Simon son of Rogo
1292	Sir Hugh de Courtenay, later Earl of Devon (d 1340)	Simon son of Rogo
ca 1300		Walter & Agnes Trenchard (after death of Ralph Colwell) sell 'Colwell Grange' to William & Genevieve de Park
1303		William & Genevieve de Park (100a)
		Bodmiscombe Hospital
1311		William & Genevieve de Park (100a) (life interest only): remainder to Philip de Courtenay
		Ralph de Colwell
		Henry Rogis son of Simon Rogis
1346	'Honour of Holcombe Rogis'	Thomas de Courtenay (9 tenths), previously owned by William de Park
		Bodmiscombe Hospital (20th part)
pre 1362/3	Sir Hugh de Courtenay, 2nd Earl of Devon (d 1377)	Sir Thomas Courtenay (d 1362) has placed Colwell (with Sutton Lucy) in trust (trustees: Hugh de Courtenay, Earl of Devon; Sir John Dinham; Roger Torell)
		?
1369		Hugh de Courtenay dies: Colwell (with Sutton Lucy) goes to his sister Margaret, later wife of Thomas Peverell (d 1422)
		?
1377	Sir Hugh de Courtenay, Earl of Devon (d 1422)	Thomas and Margaret Peverell

Date	Tenant in chief	Subtenants
		Peverell estate passes after death of Thomas & Margaret to dau Katherine wife of Sir Walter Hungerford or dau Eleanor whose heir is Robert Hungerford
1449		Robert, 2nd Lord Hungerford, inherits from uncle Sir Walter
1459	Thomas de Courtenay, Earl of Devon	Robert, 3rd Lord Hungerford, inherits from father Robert
1461	Courtenay lands confiscated after Yorkist victory	Hungerford estates forfeited & granted by Edward IV to Richard, Duke of Gloucester (later Richard III), possibly including Colwell
1464		Hungerford estates restored to Sir Thomas Hungerford, son of Robert (executed 1464)
1469	Henry Courtenay executed	Sir Thomas Hungerford executed
1481		Mary Hungerford, dau & heir of Thomas, marries Edward, Lord Hastings: their son George born c 1488
1529	Earls of Huntingdon (George Hastings created earl)	
?1560–95	Sold to William Franklin	
1614	William Collins (bp 1565) buys Colwell from the Franklin family	
1644	? Transferred to William Collins (bp 1620)	
1657	William Collins dies leaving 4 daughters as coheirs	

Table B: Owners and occupiers of Colwell Wood and Colwell Wood Cottage after 1657

Date	Owners	Occupiers
By 1680	John Mayne (d 1680)	
to 1701	Christopher Mayne (d 1701)	
1701	John Mayne (d 1726)	
1726	John Mayne (d ca 1785)	
1782–87		William Seaman
1785	Thomas Mayne sen (d 1786/7)	
1787	Thomas Mayne jun & Trustees	
1800–01		Nathaniel Stocker

Date	Owners	Occupiers
1822		John Braddick
1829		Mr Burton
1841		John Cox (Colwell Wood Cottage)
1851		John Samson (Colwell Wood Cottage)
1860	John Thomas Graves (d 1861)	
1861	12 children of John T Graves	Richard Mitchell (Colwell Wood Cottage)
1874	Sir Edward Marwood-Elton (d 1884)	
1881		(Colwell Wood Cottage unoccupied)
early 1880s		Stamp family (Colwell Wood Cottage)
1884	Revd Alfred Marwood-Elton (d 1911)	
1886		Richard Miles, gamekeeper ('Offwell Wood')
1890		Dare family (Colwell Wood Cottage)
1890–94		James Curtis (Colwell Wood Cottage)
1896–97		Mr Doswell (Colwell Wood Cottage)
1901–02		Fred Skinner (Colwell Wood Cottage)
1902–1905		William White (Colwell Wood Cottage)
1906	William Dommett sells Scrub Wood to William Elton	
1908		Thomas Sparkes (Colwell Wood dwelling)
1911	Lt-Col William Marwood-Elton inherits (d 1931). Tenant in 1911 is E J Luckock (d by May 1912)	Unoccupied in May 1912
1923–38		John Hawkins (Colwell Wood Cottage)
1931	Mrs Juliet Marwood-Elton inherits for life on death of her husband William Marwood-Elton	
1937	Mrs Marwood-Elton sells to George Blay Ltd	
1939–		Chick family (Colwell Wood Cottage)
1951		Cyril & Beatrice Brice (Colwell Wood Cottage)
1953–55		Mr Reedman (Colwell Wood Cottage)
1955–58		John Henning
1959–62		Winifred & Harry Whitham In 1961 also Nellie Silvers (d 1961)
1967		Arnold Chick (d 1982)
1985	W L Hutton	W L Hutton

Appendix B
ABSTRACTS OF DEEDS

Deed to lead the uses of a Fine
Devon Record Office 210M/T/63
24 July 1675

(1) Dorothy Collyns one of the four daughters of William Collyns late of Offwell gent
(2) John Beare the younger of Bearescombe Esq and George Beare of the same, gent

Dorothy Collyns shall before the Feast of the Annunciation next levy a *Fine sur Cognisance de droit come ceo* at the Court of Common Pleas unto John Beare and George Beare regarding
...   her quarter part of the Capital Messuage or Mansion House, Barton, Farm and demeasne lands of Collwell alias East Collwell with appurtenances
...   her quarter part of the messuage of tenement called West Collwell heretofore in the tenure of William Clapp
...   her quarter part of the Manor of Offwell
...   her quarter part of the Manor of Collwell
...   her quarter part of the Advowson of Cotleigh
...   her quarter part of the Advowson of Offwell
...   her quarter part of the moiety or the Manors of [word faded] Cullyford and Seaton
...   her quarter part of closes or meadows known as Daymond's Meadows or Corselakes meadows (10 acres) in the parish of Widworthy
...   her quarter part of closes or pastures known as Payton's Ground (8a)
...   her quarter part of that quarry or freestone and limestone in the parish of Widworthy heretofore purchased of Oliver Francklyn gent and Peter Francklyn gent or one of them
...   her quarter part of 3 messuages or tenements in Sidmouth
...   all other messuages, lands etc whereof Dorothy Collyns is seised
Signatures of John Beare, George Beare

Marriage Settlement
Devon Record Office 210M/T/64
29 September 1675

(1) Anne Collyns the younger of Collwell in the parish of Offwell, spinster, 'one of the fower daughters and coheires of William Collyns Gent deceased'
(2) John Beare the younger of Bearescombe in the said County Esq and George Beare of Bearscombe aforesaid, gent
(3) Richard Holway of Priory in the parish of Broadhembury, Devon, gent

In consideration of the forthcoming marriage of Richard Holway and Anne Collyns

Anne Collyns grants to John and George Beare

...   'all that her one Fowerth or quarter part of all the Capitall Messuage Manor House Barton Farme and Demeasne Lands of East Collwell' called or commonly known by the name of Collwell alias East Collwell...

...   her quarter part of the messuage or tenement called West Collwell heretofore in the tenure of William Clapp deceased

...   her quarter part of the Manor or Lordship of Offwell

...   her quarter part of the Manor or Lordship of Collwell

...   her quarter part of the Advowson of Cotleigh

...   her moiety or half part of the Manor of Bere in the parish of Cullyford, Devon

...   her quarter part of closes or meadows known as Daymond's Meadows or Corselakes Meadows (10 acres) in the parish of Widworthy

...   her quarter part of closes or pastures known as Payton's Ground (8a)

...   her quarter part of that quarry or freestone and limestone in the parish of Widworthy heretofore purchased of Oliver Francklyn gent and Peter Francklyn gent or one of them

...   her quarter part of 3 messuages or tenements in Sidmouth

...   all other her messuages, lands etc in Collwell, East Collwell, West Collwell, Bere, Seaton, Cullyford, Cullyton, Sidmount, Offwell, Northleigh, Widworthy and Cottleigh, and all reversions, remainders, rents etc

       All of which premises are now in the actual possession of John and George Beare, by virtue of an indenture of bargain and sale dated the day before these presents, for 10 shillings

       For the use of the said Richard Holway his heirs and assigns for ever

...   Cites *Fine sure Cognisance de droit come ceo* executed by Anne Collyns and her sister Dorothy Collyns on 28 July last at Court of Common Please unto John and George Beare by the names of the moiety of the Manor of Offwell, the moiety of the Manor of Collwell, the 4th part of the Manor of Bere and the 4th part of the Manor of Seaton, and of Cottleigh Church, and of the moiety of '30 messuages two mills 30 gardens 40 orchards 300a of land, 50a of meadow, 200a of pasture, 150a of wood, 400a of furze and heath, 50a of moor, with appurtenances, in Collwell, East Collwell, West Collwell, Bere, Seaton, Cullyford, Culliton, Sidmouth, Offwell, Northleigh, Widworthy and Cottleigh'

It is hereby declared by all parties that the said Fine shall be and ensue

Signature of Ann Collyns

Lease for a year (part of Lease and Release)
Somerset Heritage Centre DD/AY/348 (Kinglake and Newman Family Papers)
Dated 16 March 1798

(1)   Charles Lucas gentleman of New Inn, Middlesex, who survived Samuel Stennett DD of Muswell Hill, Middlesex (they being devisees and trustees of will of Thomas Mayne Esq late of Enfield, Middlesex, deceased, eldest son and heir of Walter Mayne of Colyton, deceased, eldest son of Gabriel Mayne of City of Exeter, he being the eldest son of Zachary Mayne of City of Exeter, only brother of John Mayne, merchant of City of Exeter. The testator Thomas Mayne was cousin and heir at law of John Mayne Esq, late of Kensington, Middlesex, only son and heir of John Mayne Esq, he being the son of Christopher Mayne, only son and heir of said John, brother of Zachary Mayne), and

Thomas Mayne gent of Sutton Mandeville, Wiltshire, only son and heir of said Thomas Mayne of Enfield

(2)   Thomas Graves Esq of Woodbine Hill, Combe Raleigh, Devon

Said Charles Lucas and Thomas Mayne, for 5 shillings paid to each of them by said Thomas Graves, sold all wood or woodlands called Colwell Wood in Offwell, formerly the estate of John Mayne late of Exeter, then of John Mayne of Kensington, and late of said Thomas Mayne Esq of Enfield deceased, with all timber, trees, underwood, fences, coppices, ditches, hedges, ways, paths, water-courses etc, and all profits, paying a pepper-corn rent to said Charles Lucas and Thomas Mayne

Release[144] of Colwell Wood in Offwell, Devon, in four parts
Dated 17 March 1798

Whereas John Mayne, brother of Zachary Mayne, was seized of several manors, lands and hereditaments, including the wood and hereditaments hereafter granted released, made his will on 30 May 1680, and gave his lands, manors etc to his only son Christopher Mayne for his life; Christopher enjoyed them until 1701 when he died leaving a son John Mayne, who entered the premises.

By an Indenture dated 17 October 1720 between (1) John Mayne, (2) Stephen Hodges gentleman and Thomas Craddock, gentleman, (3) Edward Bower gentleman and (4) William Gill gentleman, whereby (1) granted to (2) among other places, the manor and lordship of Colwell and Offwell with all rights etc in Offwell and Widworthy.

Reference to recoveries in Michaelmas Term 7 George I (1720) granted to said John Mayne Esq, who died intestate in 1726, leaving as his only son John Mayne Esq junior of Kensington, Middlesex. He died and his heir was his cousin Thomas Mayne late of Enfield, Middlesex. Thomas made his will on 24 September 1786, giving to his wife Mary, an annuity of £100 per annum, and to Samuel Stennett and Charles Lucas £3,000 to be raised by mortgage for his daughter Mary. His son Thomas Mayne junior inherited the property; and the will was proved on 26 March 1787 in the Prerogative Court of Canterbury by the executor Charles Lucas.

Reference to a decree in Chancery dated 18 February 1793 in a case between Thomas Mayne (Plaintiff) and said Charles Lucas and Samuel Stennett (Defendants): it was ordered that part of the estates of Thomas Mayne should be sold by auction to pay his debts and the legacies in his will. Thomas Graves was the successful bidder in the auction. By a Chancery Report of 30 April 1794 Thomas Graves paid £1,210. But on investigating the title to the woods it was supposed that recovery had been suffered by any person previous to the death of the testator Thomas Mayne in tail unaffected by the will or disposition of the testator Thomas Mayne.

Order to this effect made in Chancery on 16 April 1796.
It has since been discovered that the said John Mayne, son of Christopher Mayne, did break the entail created by his grandfather's will of 30 May 1680.
Thomas Graves, the actual purchaser, paid £1,210 into the bank for the purchase of the said woods. This conveyance vests the property in Thomas Graves.

---

[144] The release is a very lengthy document; full details of the Chancery actions and orders have not been noted.

Deeds relating to Colwell Wood (inter alia)
Somerset Heritage Centre DD/AY/349/1-5 (Kinglake and Newman Family Papers)

Lease for a year
Dated 3 December 1805
(1) Sir Thomas Graves KB, Vice-Admiral of the Blue Squadron of HM Navy
(2) Miss Mary Graves, his daughter Mary Graves spinster of Woodbine Hill parish of Combe Raleigh, near Honiton, Devon
For five shillings and out of love and affection (1) sells to (2) Woodbine Hill, Ellishayes and all the estate commonly known as Colwell Wood in parish of Urfield [*sic*] near Borough of Honiton, occupied by John Lathy
Witnesses: H R Furzer, Capt RN, Wm Davie, Attorney at Law

Release and Deed of Gift of lands and hereditaments in parishes of Combe Raleigh and Orfield [*sic*], Devon, and household furniture etc.
Dated 4 December 1805
(1) Sir Thomas Graves KB
(2) Miss Mary Graves
For ten shillings (1) sells to (2) the mansion house called Woodbine Hill and a dwelling house called Ellishayes in Combe Raleigh, and Bywood in Luppitt, and a piece of woodland commonly called Colwell Wood situate in parish of Orfield [*sic*] near Honiton, now in possession of John Lathy as tenant, with outhouses, edifices, barns, stables, courts, meadows, timber etc. Said property belongs to (1) with all deeds, furniture, plate, china, books, pictures
Witnesses: H R Furzer, Capt RN, Wm Davie, Attorney at Law

Power of Attorney dated 29 September 1870: William Taprell Graves Esq to Captain G S Graves

Certification on 25 April 1864 of Deed of Emma Jane Elizabeth, wife of Frederick William Wetherell, dated 9 January 1874, between her siblings and Sir Edward M Elton

Indenture[145] dated 9 January 1874
(1) Maria Graves widow of Lyme Regis, Dorset, George Sawle Graves late of Woodbine Hill, Combe Raleigh but now residing at Lyme Regis, a Commander in Her Majestys Royal Navy
(2) Mary Elizabeth Fetherstonhaugh Graves of Lyme Regis, spinster
(3) Catherine Anna Graves of Lyme Regis, spinster
(4) William Taprell Graves formerly of Bath, Somerset but now of Gartha Lake in the colony of New South Wales, store keeper
(5) The said George Sawle Graves
(6) Louisa Maria Graves of Lyme Regis, spinster
(7) Frederick William Wetherell of Rathmolyon, Meath, Ireland, Clerk in Holy Orders and his wife Emma Jane Elizabeth, late Graves

---

[145] This document is partially decayed, with holes (see pages 69 and 70 above); some of the text is lost.

(8) [Francis Lowry] Graves [a Lieuten]ant in Her [Majestys Royal] Artillery
(9) Alice Marianne Graves of Belmo[re] in the county of Westmeath, Ireland, spinster
(10) Somerset Henry Paul Graves, Lieutenant in her Majestys Ninth Regiment of Foot now stationed at Yarmouth
(11) Isabel Graves residing at Darmstadt in the Empire of Germany, spinster
(12) Constance Mary Graves of Lyme Regis, spinster
(13) Sir Edward Marwood Elton of Widworthy Court, Widworthy, Baronet

Whereas Mary Graves spinster late of Woodbine Hill, Combe Raleigh, made her will on 30 November 1852 with two codicils dated 2 February 1853 and 20 November 1855: after specific bequests of property in Dunkeswell (including the advowson of Dunkeswell) and other bequests, she left residue of her property to her cousins John Samuel Graves Esquire, Livingston Thompson Esquire of the City of Dublin, and Revd John Billington, Rector of Kennington, Kent, as trustees to the use of her said cousin John Samuel Graves for life, and after his death to the use of Thomas Molyneux Graves (since deceased) for life to the use of the first, second, third, fourth, fifth and every other son of the said Thomas Molyneux Graves, severally and successively one after another in seniority of age.

In the second codicil Miss Graves recited 'that she was seized of or entitled to certain freehold hereditaments situate or arising within the Parishes of Offwell and Honiton … included in the residuary d[…]vise contained in her said Will and that she was then desirous that the aforesaid hereditaments should be vested in her cousin the said John Samuel Graves …' free of limitation.

Mary Graves died on 4 March 1860, and John Samuel Graves made his will on 4 June 1860, appointing his wife Maria and son George Sawle Graves as executors. He devised his entire estate to his executors in trust for all his children, share and share alike (except the son to whom Woodbine Hill had been devised by his cousin Mary Graves; he left the household goods, cattle etc, at Woodbine Hill, to that son). John Samuel Graves died on [4 April] 1861, leaving a widow and twelve children (two others had predeceased him):

> Thomas Molyneux Graves, the eldest son (died 18 June 1855)
> George Sawle Graves
> Mary Elizabeth Featherstonhaugh Graves
> Catherine Anna Graves
> William Taprell Graves
> Emily Molyneux Graves who died an infant in about 1837
> John Samuel Graves (died 20 March 1872 intestate, a bachelor)
> Louisa Maria Graves
> Emma Jane Elizabeth Wetherell (wife of Frederick William Wetherall)
> Francis Lowry Graves
> Alice Marianne Graves
> Somerset Henry Paul Graves
> Isabel Graves
> Constance Mary Graves

The second son, George Sawle Graves, thus became the eldest surviving son and inherited Woodbine Hill.

The surviving children have now agreed with Sir Edward Marwood Elton to sell, for £136 7s 6d to each of them [section lost] … making a total of £1,500:

> 'All that estate or piece and parcel of woodland (on part whereof a cottage has been erected and other parts have been brought under cultivation) commonly called Colwell Wood situate lying and being in the parish of Offwell in the said County of Devon formerly the estate of John Mayne of the City of Exeter deceased, afterwards of John Mayne of Kensington in the County of Middlesex, deceased, then of Thomas Mayne of Enfield in the said county of Middlesex, deceased, since of Thomas Graves deceased, then of Mary Graves deceased and late of the said John Samuel Graves the testator, deceased, all which hereditaments and premises are by way of further description but not so as to bridge the grant and conveyance thereof hereinbefore made more particularly described and delineated in the plan drawn on the back of the second skin of these presents and whereon the same are colored pink. Together with all buildings commons timber and other trees underwoods fences hedges ditches wastes ways paths passages waters watercourses liberties privileges easements rights members and appurtenances whatsoever to the said hereditaments and premises belonging …'

Schedules
(1) 3 & 4 December 1805: Indentures of Lease and Release
(2) 29 September 1870: Deed Poll of William Taprell Graves
Endorsed: Conveyance of Estate called Colwell Wood from Mrs Maria Graves, George Sawle Graves Esq, and the Devisees under the will of late J S Graves, to Sir Edward M Elton
Endorsed by each of the eleven children of John Samuel and Maria Graves
Witness: John Jones. Sum received: £136 7s 3d to each of the eleven.

Deposition of George Sawle Graves Commander, RN, of Lyme Regis, Dorset
Dated 8 May 1874 at Lyme Regis

My father John Samuel Graves Esq, late of Woodbine Hill, Combe Raleigh, Devon, who died 4 April 1861, was executor of estate of his cousin Mary Graves, spinster of Woodbine Hill, who died 4 March 1860. In her will she gave my father (among other properties) an estate called Colwell Wood in parish of Offwell

I and my surviving brothers and sisters, as devisees of his will, have lately sold and conveyed same to Sir Edward Marwood Elton Bart. My siblings are as follows:

(i) & (ii) Mary Elizabeth Fetherstonhaugh Graves and Catherine Anna Graves,
      baptised 14 Nov 1830 at Tormarton, Gloucestershire
(iii)   Thomas Molyneux Graves baptised 17 September 1831 at St Martin in the Fields, London. Bachelor. Died 18 June 1855 in the Crimea
(iv)   Myself, baptised at Tormarton on 4 November 1832
(v)   William Taprell Graves baptised 2 April 1835 at Grange, Co Armagh, Ireland
(vi)   Emily Molyneux Graves baptised 12 February 1837 at Grange. Died an infant
(vii)   John Samuel Graves baptised 7 October 1838 at Grange. Died 1872
(viii)   Louisa Maria Graves baptised 28 June 1840 at Grange
(ix)   Emma Jane Elizabeth Graves (now wife of Frederick William Wetherell) baptised 11 January 1842 at Walcot, Bath

(x)   Francis Lowry Graves baptised 6 December 1843 at Walcot

(xi)   Alice Marianne Graves baptised on 23 October 1845 at Walcot

(xii)   Somerset Henry Paul Graves baptised 23 April 1847 at Walcot

(xiii)   Isabel Graves baptised 28 July 1848 at Walcot

(xiv)   Constance Mary Graves baptised 8 April 1853 at Walcot

There is no mortgage on Colwell Wood.

Deposition of Anna Lowry widow of Belmore, Co Westmeath, Ireland

Dated 17 February 1874 at Ballymore

Deponent is sister of John Samuel Graves Esq late of Woodbine, Combe Raleigh, who died 4 April 1861 at Woodbine, leaving widow Maria Graves of Lyme Regis. John Samuel Graves and Maria were married on 15 February 1827 at Charlton Kings, near Cheltenham, Gloucestershire

Children of John Samuel and Maria Graves set out [as above]

Appendix C

ABSTRACTS OF WILLS

Abstract of the Will of William Collins
Prerogative Court of Canterbury 1658
The National Archives PROB 11/273/614

William Collins of Offwell, Devon, gentleman
Dated 26 October 1657

...   Fifty shillings to be distributed by my executrix within one month next after my funeral among 'such poore people of the said parish of Offwell as my said executrix in her discretion shall thinke fit'

...   unto Zachary Chaple my Servant 40s and to Phillipp Chapple my Servant 40s

...   whereas my manors, lands tenements and hereditaments were upon my marriage with my now wife so settled that part of them after my death and the whole after my wife's death must remain and come (so I am advised) to my daughters 'who are young and of tender age and therefore have not power left in me to convey the same to such friends as I would for their best benefit during their minority, but yet being very desirous and willing that they and theire Estate should be soe disposed of and ordered as that my said daughters should be virtuously and piouslie educated and their Estate preserved and kept from wasting until they shall be of fit age and Capacitie to manage it themselves'

...   my will is that their mother would (as I am persuaded she to her utmost power will) so long as she lives see that the same be done ... and I entreat my very good friends Thomas Marwood, gentleman of Honiton, Robert Starr, gentleman of Seaton, Devon, and Andrew Ford of Offwell that they would afford her their help from time to time

...   if it shall please God to take their mother from them during their minority, my desire and earnest request unto the same is that they would be pleased to be their Guardians and take care of them and their Estate during their minorities ... and to take to themselves out of the profits of the said lands such charges as they shall be put unto and moreover I give unto them 10s apiece to buy each of them a ring

...   I give to Humphry Bradford, clerk, Rector of the parish of Offwell 50s yearly, to be paid quarterly at the birth of our Lord God, the annunciation of the blessed Virgin Mary, the nativity of St John Baptist and St Michael the Archangel, which by agreement between him and myself is to be paid and received during the life of the said Humphry Bradford while he continues Rector of the said Church, in lieu and full satisfaction of all tithes and duties whatsoever which during the said time issue or are due from one messuage or tenement with appurtenances commonly called West Colwell, otherwise Clappers Tenement, or any part thereof, in Offwell

...   to each of my female servants now living with me 12d apiece

...   to Alexander Clarke one other of my men servants 5s

...   my desire is that my father's annuity and diet agreed on between him and myself to be truly paid during his lifetime

...   residue of goods and chattels to my beloved wife Ann Collyns, whom I make executrix

Witnesses: John Sherman, William Browne
Proved 26 February 1657/8

APPENDICES

Abstract of the Will of John Mayne
Prerogative Court of Canterbury 1680
The National Archives PROB 11/367

John Mayne merchant of Exeter, Devon

... To be buried in the chancel of St Petrock's church (Exeter) should I die in Exeter, near my father and mother

... My manors, messuages, lands, tenements and hereditaments to my only son Christopher Mayne during his life, and then to his eldest son and the heirs of his body in tail; in default to my only daughter Elizabeth Mayne for her life, then to her eldest son or to her sons; in default to my brother Zachary Mayne, then to his son Gabriel Mayne for his life, and to Gabriel's eldest son; in default to Zachary's younger sons; in default of his sons to Zachary's daughters

... To son Christopher: £8,000

... To Elizabeth Wills and Sarah Wills, children of George Wills, £100 apiece when 21 or married, they marrying with consent of my brother Zachary Mayne and my executor, and my executor shall to each of them £25 to bind them as Apprentices and shall in the meantime maintain them

... To brother Zachary: £200

... To Zachary's son Gabriel Mayne: £50 per annum for seven years while he is settled and studying at any university 'the Art, Faculty, or Science of Physicke'; he to maintain his brothers and sisters out of this annuity if both their parents die and he is over 21

... If Zachary does not go to university, my executor shall pay to all Zachary's children £50 apiece 'att their respective days of marriage or placing abroad Apprentices or att their respective ages of one and Twenty'

... To daughter Elizabeth: £6,000 for her portion (assuming that she marries the son and heir of Sir Charles Woolsley with whom I have had some treaty concerning the same)

... To my said daughter, half my plate, 'my Bed now in my Purple Chamber where my late wife dyed with the Furniture now therewith used as belonging to it And my Charriott and Coach horses with the Furniture harness and Tackling to the same belonging And all the Jewells and Braceletts which were her Mother's'

... To my servant Grace Holwell £10 per annum

... To my Aunt Dorcas Penhellinke £6 per annum

... [further bequests to servants; rings worth 40s to friends]

.. £400 from personal estate for purchasing land in Exeter for a school and a house for a school master and £1,000 more to buy land near Exeter to provide a salary for the master and a writing master, and for buying books, 'to teach Boyes to read English and to write and cost accompts soe as to fit them to be Apprentices And to instruct them in the Church and the Assemblyes Catechisms', these being 40 boys of parents 'not well able to pay for their schooling' and 20 boys more whose parents may be able to pay, and no more... my name and coat of arms to be engraved in brass or stone and placed over the door. This to be done within two years, and in the meantime executor to continue to pay £40 a year, to Francis Fryer and a writing master for the purposes aforesaid

... £300 for building a school in Topsham to teach 'to read write and the Art of Navigation', provided that the inhabitants of Topsham (or someone else) makes this up to £1,000 within four years

... £200 each to towns of Dartmouth, Barnstaple and Bideford to be used for schools to teach 'reading writing ciphering and the Art of navigation', if they can raise £600 or £700 within four years

... Detailed provisions for Mayor and one Alderman of Exeter and others to administer testator's school here; brother Zachary Mayne to be among the governors

... To the poor of the parishes of St Mary Major ('St Mary the Moors'), St Sidwell, Holy Trinity, St David, St Lawrence, St John, St Paul, St Edmund, St Mary Steps and St Petrock, all in Exeter

... A monument to me to be raised in St Petrock's (cites examples to copy), Mr Ware to preach a sermon at my funeral; servants to have cloth for mourning

... Bequests of cloth for mourning to cousin Elizabeth wife of Toby Alleyn (and £100), sister of cousin Prudence Turner, cousin Toby Alleyn, Susanna Langdon daughter of Richard Mayne late of City of Exeter and sister of Richard Mayne (£10), Elizabeth Clarke, Susanna Fox, Mary Stone, cousins Andrew Quash, John Warren, Henry Quash of Taunton, and other members of Quash family, cousin Thomas Turner, mother in law Faith Ceely, 'my brother Thomas Ceely', uncle Oliver Ceely and his wife Ann, cousin John Ceely of Exeter, cousins John Starr and Anne Pate

... Residue to son Christopher, he to be executor

Overseers: Roger Tuckfield junior of Exeter, George Ceely, John Ceely of Plymouth, brother Zachary Mayne, Thomas Turner, Toby Alleyn and William Farrer

Dated 30 May 1680

Witnesses: John Carter, Samuel Gibbeard, John Collier, Peter Ceely

Proved 29 June 1680

Abstract of the Will of Thomas Mayne
Prerogative Court of Canterbury 1787
The National Archives PROB 11/1157

Thomas Mayne of Middle Temple Lane, London

... By the death of John Mayne esquire late of Kensington, I became entitled to considerable real estate

... To my wife Mary Mayne: annuity of £100 per annum to be paid out of my estate called 'Cheeks Grove', Wiltshire

... To my friends Mr Samuel Stennett of Muswell Hill, Middlesex, and Mr Charles Lucas of New Inn, Middlesex: £3,000 to be raised by sale or mortgage of any other part of my real estate; this sum to be invested in stocks etc and interest to be paid to my daughter Mary for her life; after her decease, the same to be divided between her children and grandchildren

... To my said trustees: my estate called Cheeks Grove and all my other freehold estates, to be sold and to raise £3,000 and to permit my son Thomas Mayne to take rents and profits for his life; in default to my daughter Mary and her issue

 (extensive powers to trustees to make leases; my son Thomas can grant by deed property not exceeding £500 to any wife he may marry)

... To my wife and to my said daughter Mary: £50 each

... To my brothers John and Gabriel Mayne: £50 each

... To Mary Gay, the only child of said daughter Mary: £500 when 21 or married and until then the same to be laid out for her education and maintenance

... To Mrs Margaret Pope and Mr Joshua Pope: £50 each for mourning

... To Mary Dandy, my said wife's daughter by a former husband: £100 when 21

... To the trustees: £200 each

... Residue to my son Thomas, he and the trustees to be executors

Will dated 24 September 1786

Witnesses: Nathl Goodridge, Richard Gunner, Willm Hepburn

Codicil: legacy to daughter increased to £4,000. Dated 26 March 1787

Witnesses: Joshua Blower Nevill, Joel Mayne, James Carnall

Codicil: to John and Elizabeth Dandy, children of my wife Mary: £100 each when 21, to be laid out for them until then for their maintenance and education
To wife: all furniture, plate, linen and china for life and after her death to such of her children (Mary Dandy, John Dandy and Elizabeth Dandy) as shall be living
Dated 26 March 1787. Witnesses: Joshua Blower Nevill, Joel Mayne, James Carnall

Appeared Personally: Charles Lucas gentleman of New Inn, Middlesex. Testator was formerly of the Middle Temple Lane, but late of Ponders End, parish of Enfield, Middlesex. An error in 2nd codicil re the name of one of the children of testator's wife was immediately corrected by Charles Lucas.
Proved 25 September 1787

Abstract of the Will of Henry Southcott
Prerogative Court of Canterbury 1706
The National Archives PROB 11/491/81

Henry Southcott gentleman of Offwell, Devon
Dated 1 Apr 1706

...   My body to be decently interred in the Parish Church of Offwell the Vault to be enlarged 'that I may lye by the side of my deceased wife'

...   To the poor of the Parish of Offwell £20, the interest to be 'to such poore people of the said Parish who by reason of their poverty and hard labour doe keep themselves from the relief of the said Parish', to be distributed once a year on the 25 December amongst 'such poor people as above expressed at the election of four of the best of the Parish of Offwell

...   To Elizabeth Beare £10, to Francis Bear £10, to Thomas Bear £10, sons and daughters of John Bear and Mary his wife of Bearescombe

...   To Mr George Saffin the son of Mrs Mary Saffin £100

...   To Mrs Dorothy Saffin £100, to Mrs Mary Saffin, daughters of Mrs Mary Saffin, £100

...   To Edward Wood's eldest son £10

...   To my sister Mrs Mary Saffin £30

To Mrs Mary Ponsford my niece £10

To Mr William Ponsford his wife's picture

...   To Mr George Southcott of Dowleshayse son of Mr Thomas Southcott my Fairs and Markets of Axminster

To Mrs Saffin my sister 'my cellar Cabanet my silver porringer'

...   To Mrs Mary Saffin my niece and to Mrs Dorothy Saffin my silver plate with my wife's coat [of arms] in the middle

To Mr George Saffin my watch

To Mrs Elizabeth Ponsford my two silver cups

...   To Luke Pitman £5

To Mary Long £5

To the Right Honble Thomas Lord Petre and to his Lady and son and daughter to each a gold ring

To Mr Birch and Mr Williamson a gold ring to each

To my Cook Maid 20s

To Susan Batt 20s

... The residue of personal estate to my brother Mr Thomas Southcott of Dowleshayse, whom I appoint sole executor

... To Luke Pitman and to Mary Long a Cow to each

Witnesses: William Brown, Alexander Long, Nathaniel Spocker

Proved 8 November 1706

Abstract of the Will of John Samuel Graves
Principal Probate Registry 1861

John Samuel Graves late of Woodbine Hill in the parish of Combe Raleigh
'written at Bath but I hope will be executed in London tomorrow'

... My wife to be executrix & my son George Sawle Graves executor

... The former during her widowhood and the latter after her death or second marriage, guardian of my minor children

... Whereas I am trustee to my son Somerset Henry Paul Graves of £500 in 3 per cent consols, the interest of which is bequeathed to me for his education, the principal to be paid to him at 21

... All my real and personal estate to my executor and executrix in trust for all my children except that son to whom Woodbine Hill has been devised by my cousin's will but I leave to that son all the furniture, plate, linen, pictures, stock of cattle and farming implements which may be at Woodbine Hill at the time of my death

Witnesses: Emma Molyneaux of Castledillon
              Elizabeth Molyneaux daughter of the above

Made at Folkstone 4 June 1860

Testator died 4 April 1861 at Woodbine Hill

Proved 23 May 1861 on oath of Maria Graves, widow, of Woodbine Hill, power reserved to George Sawle Graves. Effects under £4,000

Resworn at the Stamp Office, October 1863, under £7,000

Renunciation of George Sawle Graves the other executor dated September 1878; filed 20 December 1878 at Exeter

Appendix D

ADMIRAL SIR THOMAS GRAVES

Thomas Graves was born in about 1747, the third son of the Revd John Graves of Castledawson, County Londonderry, and joined the Royal Navy at a very early age, serving first under his uncle, Admiral Samuel Graves (1713–1787), in the Seven Years' War (1757–63). He was first cousin once removed to Admiral Thomas, Baron Graves (?1725–1802). His three brothers also joined the Navy and served as captains, being appointed admirals on the superannuated list.

In peacetime Thomas was appointed with his cousin, Admiral Thomas Graves, to the *Antelope*; under his cousin's command he was promoted to lieutenant of the *Shannon* in 1765, when he was not yet 20 years old. He continued as lieutenant of the *Arethusa* in 1770, and in 1773 he was appointed to the *Racehorse* with Captain Constantine Phipps, making an exploratory expedition to the Arctic Seas.

In 1774 Graves went to North America with his uncle, where he commanded the small schooner *Diana*, with 30 men, which was employed to prevent smuggling. On 27 May 1775 the *Diana* was sent into the Charles River, where she was attacked by a large force of rebels with two field guns. Greatly outnumbered, the ship was eventually grounded and set alight by the insurgents. Graves was badly burned, along with his brother John who was serving as lieutenant on one of the boats sent to assist the *Diana*.

Graves continued to serve in America for several years and commanded the sloop *Savage* in 1779. He had command of the *Bedford* at the Battle of Chesapeake in September 1781, and in the following year saw much action against the French in the Caribbean including a severe action on the *Magicienne* with the much larger French frigate *Sybille*, a battle that left both ships wrecked.

When peace returned in 1783 Graves spent some time in France, and did not see action again until October 1800 when he was appointed Captain of the *Cumberland*, serving under Lord St Vincent in the English Channel. In January 1801 he was promoted to rear-admiral of the white, and he was second in command to Lord Nelson on board the *Defiance* at the Battle of Copenhagen on 2 April 1801, the purpose of which was to keep the Baltic open for essential British naval supplies; an armed neutrality between Denmark, Sweden and Russia (who supported France) raised concerns that these lines of supply would be blockaded. Diplomatic approaches having failed, it was agreed to attack the Danish fleet at Copenhagen. The attack began at 10.05 and the *Defiance* was soon stranded; Nelson disregarded a signal from Sir Hyde Parker, the commander-in-chief, to discontinue battle (he is famously said to have raised his telescope to his blind eye and said 'I really do not see the signal'). The bombardment continued and both sides suffered heavy casualties.[146] A ceasefire was eventually agreed and Nelson went on shore to negotiate a 14-week armistice.

---

[146] Accounts of the numbers vary widely (Graves initially thought the British had lost only 90), but British losses appear to have been in the region of 250 and Danish losses closer to 800.

In describing the battle, *The Times* described Admiral Graves as 'a very gallant fellow':

The Edgar led on to the attack, followed by the Ardent, Isis, Glatton, Elephant (Lord Nelson), Ganges, Defiance (Admiral Graves, a very gallant fellow), Monarch, Bellona (got on shore), Polyphemus, and Russel (ran on shore), who all anchored as they arrived up... The Enemy made a very obstinate resistance, and fought like brave men. The action continued without an interval for five hours. Most of our ships are very cut up, and we have a number of killed and wounded, amounting to nearly four hundred. The Defiance, Monarch and Isis are the principal sufferers... it was the most dreadfully fought action that took place in the annals of history...

... The Defiance's loss was principally caused by her grounding opposite to the Crown Battery, which opened full upon her; and the failure of the other ships getting in their stations...[147]

We also have Thomas Graves' own account of the battle, in a letter written on the following day to his brother John Graves of Exeter, which conveys both his awe and compassion at the scale of the battle and his relish of the excitement:

Yesterday an awful day for the town of Copenhagen ... It was, certainly, a most gallant defence, and words cannot speak too high of the boldness of the attack, considering all the difficulties we had to struggle with, and their great superiority in number and weight of guns... I fear we shall not have much to boast of when it is known what our ships suffered, and the little impression we made on their navy...

Lord Nelson ... asked for me to serve with him; if not, you might depend on my not staying behind when anything was to be done. I think yesterday must prove that the enterprise of the British is invincible...

Lord Nelson sent for me at the close of the action, and it was beautiful to see how the shot beat the water all round us in the boat. Give my love to my dear daughter. She has ever the most ardent prayers for her happiness. The destruction amongst the enemy is dreadful. One of the ships that was towed into the fleet yesterday had between two and three hundred dead on her decks, besides what they had thrown overboard.[148]

The Times, and Lord Nelson, thought that Graves should be made a baronet for his part in this ferocious battle. He received a vote of thanks from Parliament and a knighthood was given to him on the quarterdeck of the *St George* by Lord Nelson.

Despite poor health Graves remained in active service until January 1802, and in 1804 and 1805 he was third in command at the blockade of Brest. On 9 November 1805 he was promoted to Vice-Admiral, whereupon (there being too many others in this rank) he was removed from office, and he retired with reluctance to his house Woodbine Hill, near Honiton, Devon, which he had built in 1798. On 2 August 1812 he was finally promoted to Admiral.

---

[147] 'Extract of a letter from an officer, dated Copenhagen Roads, April 5', *The Times*, 20 April 1801.
[148] Letter from Admiral Sir Thomas Graves to John Graves of Barley House, Exeter, 3 April 1801.

Sir Thomas married twice, but had only one child, Mary. He died in 1814 at Woodbine Hill. Since he made no will, letters of administration in respect of his estate were granted to his daughter, Mary, on 2 August 1815, his widow Susanna having renounced her right to act as administrator of his personal estate, which was worth about £1,500. There is a memorial to Admiral Sir Thomas Graves and later members of his family in the church at Combe Raleigh, the parish in which Woodbine Hill lay (see Chapter Four).

The portrait of Sir Thomas Graves by James Northcote (see above, page 49) was hung in No 10 Downing Street by the then Prime Minister Margaret Thatcher (later Baroness Margaret Thatcher), and remained there during the tenure of her successor Sir John Major. It replaced a Gainsborough portrait entitled 'Lady in Blue'. The following photograph was signed by Sir John Major and presented to W L Hutton of Colwell Wood Cottage (thanks to the then Guernsey Lt Governor, Vice-Admiral Sir John Coward).

John Major's Cabinet in July 1996 with the Northcote portrait of Sir Thomas Graves behind

Appendix E

VIRGINIA DARE

The history of the doomed attempt to establish a colony at Roanoke Island is shrouded in mystery and uncertainty. Over the centuries there has been a huge amount of speculation about the fate of the colonists, but we shall begin by setting out what is reliably known from contemporary sources.

After a first failed attempt in 1585, Sir Walter Raleigh sent out 117 new settlers from London to Roanoke in July 1587 under the pioneer and draughtsman John White, who was appointed Governor of the colony. Among those whom White transported was his married daughter Eleanor and her husband Ananias Dare, who was a London merchant and one of the 'Assistants' or leaders of the colony. From the list of children in the colony it is clear that no children of their own accompanied them when they emigrated. The colonists arrived at Hatorask on 22 July and from there went to Roanoke. On 18 August Eleanor gave birth to a daughter who was named Virginia; she was the first English child born in North America. Among the colonists was a priest (whose name is unknown) and on 20 August 1587 he wrote:

> Eleanor daughter to the Governor and wife of Ananias Dare, one of the Assistants, was delivered of a daughter in Roanoke and the same was christened there the Sunday following and because this child was the first Christian born in Virginia she was named Virginia.[149]

A week later, on 27 August, Governor John White, rather against his better judgment, was persuaded to return to England to request supplies. He promised to return to Roanoke within three months, and after a difficult journey arrived at Southampton on 8 November. Several factors, including the Spanish Armada, prevented his return and it was not until three years before he set foot again at Roanoke. In 1590 he found no surviving settlers, just a few rusty cannons and some old water-soaked charts.

No good contemporary evidence has ever been found to explain what happened to the 117 colonists, but the most likely explanation is that they were all murdered by local native Indians. On his return White found the word 'Croatoan' carved into a post at the deserted fort, and the letters 'CRO' carved into a nearby tree; these clues suggest that the colonists may have attached themselves to local Croatoan Indians. If they were not all murdered, it has also been suggested that the surviving colonists sought shelter with, or attached themselves to, the Chowanac or Hatteras Indian tribes. In 1607 the colonist John Smith of Jamestown, Virginia, attempted to discover what became of the Roanoke settlers, but he made no headway. In truth we have no convincing evidence about the fate of the colonists after August 1587.

In September 1937 a tourist visiting the east bank of the Chowan River, Chowan County, North Carolina, stumbled upon a granite stone, weighing about 21 pounds and measuring 14 by 10 inches.

---

[149] E Clowes Chorley, 'The Planting of the church in Virginia', *William & Mary College Quarterly*, 2nd Series, vol 10, 1930, page 195.

On one side there was a Latin cross beneath which it was written: 'Ananias & Virginia Dare went hence unto Heaven 1591' and 'Anye Englishman shew John White Govr. Via'. On the reverse there were 17 lines of writing purporting to tell the fate of Raleigh's 'Lost Colony', which can be summarised as follows: after John White left for England in August 1587 the colonists came to Chowan region, suffered misery and war for four years and were reduced to 24 survivors. In 1591 the Indians heard that a ship had arrived in Roanoke, and soon after, incited by their priests, the Indians murdered all but seven of the colonists, Ananias and Virginia Dare being among the victims. The massacred colonists were buried four miles east of Chowan on a small hill on which a rock is placed with their names. The message ends with the offer of a reward to anyone who will inform Governor White and lead him to the surviving colonists, and was signed with the initials E.W.D. which is believed to stand for Eleanor White Dare.[150]

Opinion was divided as to whether this extraordinary discovery was a hoax or genuine. However, in the following four years no less 48 further similar carved stones were found in the Carolinas and as far away as Georgia. One of these stones, dated 1598, asserted that Eleanor had married the King of the Nacoochee tribe; another says that she had daughter by him. Another stone stated that Eleanor Dare was now dead, leaving behind a daughter called Agnes. Although we have not investigated all the 'messages' on the stones, there is no report that Virginia Dare survived after 1591 or had any descendants. The great majority of academic experts dismiss the 'Dare Stones' as fabrications and frauds, and it is certainly very surprising that none was discovered before 1937. The stones are just one aspect of the great mythology, fiction and speculation that has grown up around Virginia Dare. There are other traditions and speculations which assert that the colonists who not massacred (including a young woman) married into local Indian tribes and left descendants, but there are no hard facts to support any of these theories.

Even if Virginia had survived and left descendants (which is extremely unlikely), they would not have had the surname Dare. Thus any connection with the Dare family of Colwell would be through any son, nephew or kinsman Ananias might have had. Many published sources[151] state that Ananias was a tiler and bricklayer by trade; we have not found the contemporary evidence for this, but it is plausible, since such a practical trade would have been a very great asset for building the colony's houses.

Ananias Dare and Eleanor White ('Elinor Whyte') married at the parish church of St Clement Danes, Westminster, on 24 June 1583, probably after the reading of banns. No record has been found of the baptisms of any children born in England, but there were two grants of administration for the estate of Ananias Dare, after it had been assumed that he had died in Virginia, by the Prerogative Court of Canterbury, which had jurisdiction over the estates of those who died *in p[ar]tibus ultra marinis* (overseas). The second of these, dated 27 June 1597, was recorded as follows:

> Administration of estate of Ananias Dare, formerly of parish of St Bride, City of London, granted to John Nokes, kinsman, to administer goods during the minority of son John Dare, following previous grant of 24 April 1594 to Robert Sachfeild, who renounces.

---

[150] 'Dare Stone', *Dictionary of America History*, edited James Truslow Adams (Vol 2, London, 1940).
[151] Eg Lee Miller, *Roanoke: Solving the Mystery of the Lost Colony* (Penguin Books, 2002).

From this we learn that Ananias had a son called John Dare, who was a minor, and in effect John Nokes acted as his trustee during his minority. Unfortunately, the parish registers of St Bride's only survive from 1653; assuming that John was born there, there will be no surviving record of his baptism, and equally if he married there and had children of his own baptised at St Bride's, there will be no record. It is clear that the boy John Dare was still living in 1597, and thus he was presumably left behind when his parents or father emigrated in 1587.

Further investigation of probate sources indicates that the surname Dare was heavily concentrated in east Devon and the adjoining western tip of Dorset, and in the sixteenth century there were prosperous Dare families at Upottery and Seaton, both of which are close to Colwell. We may speculate that William Dare (born circa 1765, died 1835), miller of Colwell Mill (see above, page 76), was possibly descended from one of these testators, but further work would need to be carried out to establish this with certainty.

Appendix F
SALE PARTICULARS

DEVONSHIRE

Close to the excellent market towns of Honiton and Axminster, on the main Southern Railway
Line, and within easy distance of the South Coast Resorts of Seaton, Sidmouth and Lyme Regis

PARTICULARS

WITH PLANS AND CONDITIONS OF SALE

of

The Outlying Portions of

The Widworthy Estate

comprising

EIGHT VALUABLE FARMS & HOLDINGS

With good Farmhouses and Homesteads

SEVERAL EXCELLENT COTTAGES

ACCOMMODATION LANDS

BUILDING SITES AND WOODLANDS

situated in the Parishes of Widworthy, Offwell, Colyton, Dalwood and Shute.

The whole extending to an area of about

1,350 Acres

WHICH

DAVIS, CHAMPION & PAYNE

Are instructed to Sell by Auction

AT " THE DOLPHIN HOTEL," HONITON

On TUESDAY, JULY 6th, 1937
punctually at 3 p.m.

Copies of these Particulars may be obtained from the Auctioneers, 16 Kendrick Street,
Stroud, Glos., Tel. 675/676, or from Messrs TWEED & SON, Solicitors, Honiton, Devon

Stroud News

LOT 22

(Coloured blue on plan No. 5)

A Valuable Area of Woodland

known as

COLWELL WOOD

situate in the Parish of Offwell with an approach from the Offwell Road.

The Wood contains a quantity of matured timber and young plantations of oak, beech, etc. The whole extends to an area of approximately

69 Acres

of which the following is a Schedule taken from the Ordnance Survey Map.

SCHEDULE

No. on O.S.M.		Description				Acreage
359	Pt. Colwell Wood	Woodland	..	..	..	7·661
196	Pt. Do.	Do.	..	..	..	40·155
163	Plot	.. ..	..	..	..	1·368
162	Do.	.. ..	..	..	..	·956
161	Site	Building	..	..	..	·263
90	Pt. of Colwell Wood	Woodland	..	..	..	3·444
153	Scrub Wood	Do	..	..	..	2·272
154	Do. .	Do.	..	..	..	11·877
155	Spring	Do.	..	..	..	·702
164	Pheasantry	Do.	..	..	..	·302
						69·000

This lot is sold subject to all existing rights of way.

Vacant Possession will be given on Completion.

27

BIBLIOGRAPHY

Published Sources

Medieval

Calendar of Inquisitions Post Mortem. Volume 3, Edward I (HMSO, 1912).

Calendar of Inquisitions Post Mortem. Volume 14, Edward III (HMSO, 1912).

Calendar of Inquisitions Post Mortem. Volume 22, Henry VI (Woodbridge: Boydell & Brewer: 2003).

Calendar of the Fine Rolls preserved in the Public Record Office. Volume 8, Edward III 1369–1377 (HMSO, 1911).

Calendar of the Fine Rolls preserved in the Public Record Office. Volume 19, Henry VI 1452–1461 (HMSO, 1911).

Devon Feet of Fines. Volume 2: 1272–1369 (Devon & Cornwall Record Society: Exeter, 1939).

J E B Gover, A Mawer & F M Stenton, *The Place-Names of Devon* (Cambridge, 1932).

Judith A Green, 'Baldwin [Baldwin de Meulles] (d.1086x90)', *Oxford Dictionary of National Biography*, (Oxford University Press, 2004).

History of Parliament: House of Commons 1386–1421 (Alan Sutton: Stroud, 1993).

Inquisitions and Assessments relating to Feudal Aids (HMSO, 1899).

Liber Feodorum: The Book of Fees, commonly called Testa de Nevill, reformed from the Earliest MSS (HMSO, 1920, 1923).

Vera C M London, ed, *The Cartulary of Canonleigh Abbey* (Devon & Cornwall Record Society, new series, vol 8, 1965).

Charles Ross, *Edward IV* (London, 1974).

Caroline Thorn and Agnes O'Driscoll, eds, *Domesday Book, Volume 9: Devon* (Phillimore: Chichester, 1985).

Genealogical and Biographical

Burke's Peerage and Baronetage (London: 1894, 1970).

Burke's Landed Gentry (London: 1937, 1939, 1952).

G E Cokayne, *The Complete Peerage of England, Scotland, Ireland, Great Britain and the United Kingdom, extant, extinct or dormant* (12 volumes, 1910–1959; reproduced by Alan Sutton in 6 volumes: Gloucester, 1987).

Frederick Thomas Colby, ed, *The Publications of the Harleian Society, volume 6: The Visitation of the County of Devon in the Year 1620* (London, England: Taylor & Co, 1872).

BIBLIOGRAPHY

William James Copleston, *Memoir of Edward Copleston, DD, Bishop of Llandaff* (London, 1851).

Debrett's Illustrated Baronetage and Knightage (London, 1865).

Foster's Peerage (1870).

Gentleman's Magazine 1814, 1816.

J K Laughton, 'Graves, Sir Thomas (*c* 1747–1814), revised by J D Davies, *Oxford Dictionary of National Biography* (Oxford University Press, 2004)

Lodge's Peerage, Baronetage and Knightage (1912).

'The Marwoods of Honiton and Colyton, Part I', *Devon & Cornwall Notes & Queries*, vol 32 (1971–73) pp 48–51.

Bertha Porter, 'Mayne, Zachary (1631–1694)', revised by H J McLachlan, *Oxford Dictionary of National Biography* (Oxford University Press, 2004).

Ann Sheridan, 'Zachary Mayne 1631–1694' *Transactions of the Devon Association*, vol 126 (1994), pages 181–197.

Local and County Histories

Leonard E Braddick, 'The Port of Topsham: its ships and shipbuilding', *Transactions of the Devon Association*, vol 85 (1953).

A History of Offwell Church and Parish (Debrett Ancestry Research, 2009).

W G Hoskins, *Devon* (1954, revised 2003).

Kelly's Directory of Devon(shire), various editions, 1883–1935.

Samuel & Daniel Lysons, *Magna Britannica* (1822).

Sir William Pole, *Collections towards a Description of the County of Devon* (London, 1791).

Richard Polwhele, *The History of Devonshire in Three Volumes* (1793–1806).

Clive N Ponsford, ed, *Shipbuilding on the Exe: The Memoranda Book of Daniel Bishop Davy (1799–1874)* (Devon and Cornwall Record Society, new series, vol 31, 1988).

Tristram Risdon, *Chronographical Description or Survey of Devon*. (17th century; first printed in garbled form, 1714; first good edition 1811).

D McNee Stirling, *The Beauties of the Shore: A Guide to the Watering-Places of the South-East Coast of Devon* (1838).

J R Tarling, 'Building Raynes Park', Raynes Park and West Barnes Residents' Association website.

William White, *History, Gazetteer and Directory of Devonshire* 1878–79.

Newspapers

Devon and Exeter Gazette, various editions.

Exeter Flying Post, 2 May 1786.

Exeter and Plymouth Gazette, various editions.

Express & Echo 19 & 23 September 1938.

The Times, 20 April 1801.

Western Times, various editions.

BIBLIOGRAPHY

Miscellaneous
Diary of Walter Yonge, MP for Honiton ... 1604–1628 (London: Camden Society 1848).
J W Norie, *The Shipwright's Vade-Mecum* (1822).
Ordnance Survey Maps 1809, 1888, 1906 (National Library of Scotland).
Surveyors' Drawings for the Ordnance Survey One-inch Map (1809), British Library.
Daniel J Franklin, 'The Productive Potential of Ancient Oak-Coppice Woodland in Britain',
    Rural Development Forestry Network Paper 15d (Summer 1993).

Unpublished Sources

Cornwall Record Office, Truro
Exchequer Memoranda Roll, Easter Term 1383.
    (copy in Arundell papers, Cornwall Record Office AR1/912).

Devon Record Office, Exeter
Offwell Parish Registers (364A/PR/1).
Seating plan, Offwell church (PR517/160).
Offwell Churchwardens Accounts 1691–1868 (364A/PW1–3).
Electoral registers for Offwell 1832–1962.
Tithe map and award for Offwell 1842–45 (364A/PB 1–2).
Sale particulars, 1919 (547B/P1836), 1937 (547B/p/3828/i).
Land tax returns for Offwell 1780–1832.
Miscellaneous letters to Bishop Copleston (1149/F24).
Manorial survey c1793 (Culbeare) (924B/E5/3).
Miscellaneous deeds and papers (210M/T/92–101).
Marwood Elton Collection (281M).
John C Tingey, 'Calendar of Deeds Enrolled within the County of Devon' (typed abstracts).
Surgeon's Licence: Petition from John Copleston and the Rector of Offwell re
    Zachary Chapple, [1662–1667], Diocesan Records.

General Register Office for England and Wales
Certificates:
    Birth of Thomas Alfred Sweetland 1888.
    Marriage of Thomas Dare and Amanda Susan White 1888.
    Birth of Frank Dare 1890.
    Marriage of Frank Dare and Alice Mary Ann Stamp 1913.
    Birth of Evelyn Amanda Dare 1913.

BIBLIOGRAPHY

The National Archives, London
Discovery Catalogue: Abstracts of Chancery Proceedings.
Prerogative Court of Canterbury Wills:
1662   Samuel Mayne (PROB 11/307/275).
      1680   John Mayne (PROB 11/367).
      1787   Thomas Mayne (PROB 11/157).
      1706   Henry Southcott (PROB 11/491).
      1646   Richard Mayne (PROB 11/199).
      1695   Zachary Mayne (PROB 11/426).
Census Returns of Offwell 1841–1911.
Chancery Proceedings: 1739 (C 11/657/7); 1758 to 1800 (C12 184/10).
Inquisition Post Mortem: Hugh de Curtenay 1292 (C133/62).
Inland Revenue Estate Duty Register (IR 27/194).
Inland Revenue Valuation Office Field Books: Exeter (Offwell) (IR 58/30470).
Admirals' Logs (ADM 53).
Captains' Logs (ADM 51/757, ADM 51/4127).
Captains' Letters (ADM 1 1839–1840).

Principal Probate Registry, London
Principal Probate Registry Wills:
      1860   Mary Graves.
      1861   John Samuel Graves.

Somerset Record Office, Taunton
Kinglake and Newman Family Papers:
      DD\AY/348/1–3 (1798): Purchase of Colwell Wood in Offwell, with plan.
      DD\AY/349/1–5 (1805–1874): 'Conveyance by Sir Thomas Graves to his daughter Mary
      of Woodbine Hill and Ellishayes in Coombe Rawleigh, Bywood Meadow
      in Luppitt and Colwell Wood in Offwell, 1805, map of Colwell Wood with table of
      references, 1838; power of attorney William Taprell Graves to Capt. Geo. Sawle
      Graves; 1870 and sale by Maria Graves and Geo Sawle Graves to Sir Edward
      Marwood Elton of estate called Colwell in Offwell, endorsed with map of Colwell
      Wood, 1874'.

West Country Studies Library, Exeter
Lieutenant-Colonel J V Ramsden, 'A Parochial History of Offwell and Widworthy'
      (Honiton, 1946: unpublished typescript).
Burnett Morris Index.
Miscellaneous Series.
Draft agreement for remise and quitclaim 1590–1608 (T4).

BIBLIOGRAPHY

London Metropolitan Archives, London
Parish Registers of St Alphege, Greenwich: Marriages 1771.

Dorset Record Office
Manorial Valuation 1544/5 (D16/M114).

Miscellaneous
Information kindly supplied by Mr Bob Stamp and Mrs Evelyn Sweetland.
Family Search (Church of Jesus Christ of Latter-day Saints, online: incorporates
and supersedes the *International Genealogical Index*).

INDEX

Numbers in italics refer to illustrations.

Printed in Great Britain
by Amazon